HAUNTED HEIRLOOMS

ANNA MARIA MANALO

BEYOND THE FRAY

Publishing

CONTENTS

PART III
THE LITHOGRAPH

PART IV
THE FURNITURE ROOM

PART V
THE BARRISTER'S BOOKCASE

BEYOND THE FRAY

Publishing

ACKNOWLEDGMENTS

I would like to thank the antique dealers and their families and friends who helped them to remember the encounters outlined in this book. For some it was a voyage into sinister territory which cost them sleepless nights, a sense of isolation and what was an unraveling of what serenity and routine they had in their lives. For others, it made them pause and reflect on what bonded people to the heirlooms they loved and how a tragic death may have forged a tear in the fabric of reality, allowing events such as these to occur.

A few chose to retire within months of these uncanny events, and some stayed on, now wary of signs and signals that what they have in their hands and shops may still remain in the hearts of the dead.

I would like to thank my publishers, G. Michael Hopf and Shannon LeGro of Beyond the Fray Publishing, the editors and the talented cover artist who made this book a reality.

Thank you to my husband, Wally, and my dog, Quentin, for putting up with my hours of solitude while they awaited dinner and a walk, not in that order.

Last but not least, thank you to my readers for purchasing this book. When you have a chance, please kindly remember that your reviews on Amazon are important to me as an author.

～

To share your own story:

Follow me on Facebook or email me at Cinescriber@gmail.com. Should your story be considered, you will receive a signed copy of my book and the knowledge that your story may reach thousands and change their perception of reality forever.

For updates:

Follow me on Amazon or subscribe to my website at http://www.storyartisan.wordpress.com.

For weekly true stories of the macabre:

Follow THE SINISTER ARCHIVES podcast. Available on Amazon audible, Google Podcast, Spotify, Spreaker, IHeartRadio, Podchaser and YouTube.

FOREWORD
JIM HAROLD

I have always loved thrifting, but my enthusiasm has been dampened a bit in recent years. First, while I love antiques, my dear wife, Dar, classifies most as "old junk." While I vociferously disagree with this, she has an excellent eye for interior design, and I mostly go with her thinking about furnishing our home. Though I believe antiques can be quite lovely when artistically placed together in a room, I am not anyone's idea of an interior designer.

Still, that's not the main reason I've become less of a collector in my middle age. The other reason is a bit more sinister. I am a professional podcaster who has done over 2,000 episodes of programs dealing with the supernatural. In this time, I have interviewed great thinkers on the questions of hauntings and haunted objects. Guests like the late, great Rosemary Ellen Guiley and the *Haunted Collector* himself, John Zaffis, have appeared on *The Paranormal Podcast.* These and others have brought great light to heirlooms that come along with something a little extra.

Also, on my show *Jim Harold's Campfire,* I have interviewed many experiencers about their encounters with haunted objects.

Stories have included the Ouija board that "walked" across a floor and refused to burn in a fireplace. Or that of a young girl terrorized by a lamp in the form of a female flamenco dancer who would come alive at night to traumatize the young victim.

These harrowing accounts and my wife's resistance have significantly reduced my acquisition of antiques. First, I believe my wife might draw up papers should I bring too many old items into our home. More to the point, I think I might *actually bring something into our home!*

This is why I was thrilled when Anna Maria Manalo asked me to write the foreword to *Haunted Heirlooms. The subject resonates with me.* In these pages, you will find Anna Maria's and others' accounts about their encounters with extremely haunted objects.

What I found most compelling here were the stories from antique aficionados who are not easily spooked by old items. They've likely seen, held, bought, and sold thousands of them. However, as you will soon learn, each, in their own way, was impacted profoundly by their *Haunted Heirloom* experience.

Enjoy Anna Maria's stellar work here. Then, when you visit that quaint little antique store next time, consider what spiritual stowaways might be riding along when you take that great "bargain" home.

– Jim Harold, Host of *Jim Harold's Campfire & The Paranormal Podcast* April 2022

INTRODUCTION

An unceasing wanderlust to travel the world seized me while on an escorted tour of Italy after college graduation. It went on from that first European trip with a school friend in tow, to several trips overseas, finally well into my forties and to now. I unwittingly met locals and travelers alike who regaled me with their stories during overnight stops, dinners and the like. I subsisted on travel photography jaunts at some point, taking on assignments that led me to the most cultural spots on earth.

By the time I was in my early fifties, I had decided to take the opportunity to leave my tenure as a change of venue, seeing myself stunted if not outright appalled by an archaic environment that presented ironically as a public school system. That rigid mentality suppressed my deep desire to remain creative and open to new ideas and worlds.

So here I am, a scribe of books, largely based on accounts shared with me from parts of the globe, parts of my adoptive country and regions of the Philippines, my country of birth. Some are historical, some contemporary, but nevertheless rich with atmosphere, strangeness and inexplicability. They're a part of our world that remains hidden until a tragedy opens them to view.

This particular book you have in your hands concentrates on the states collectively referred to as New England, where I resided in the late '70s as a teen and later as a young college coed. I thank God for imparting to me a discerning eye for a riveting story that awaits telling, as well as the ability to tease it out of the original storyteller. It was inspired by my first encounter with an antique piece of furniture, which I obtained from a dubious vendor. I was studying at a small Jesuit university at the time with a budding desire to own vintage furniture, objets d'art and fine bone china.

It isn't often that an interest would stay with me long from year to year or decade to decade as I matured, but among those, the joy of perusing antiques stayed with me, as I loved beautiful objects and superb craftsmanship. My passion to travel to far-flung destinations and to seek distinctive objects led me to meet some interesting, often highly educated or self-educated and erudite individuals who had circled the globe themselves. While an independent travel photographer, I had the privilege to meet well-read, informative and inquisitive individuals: some imparted stories that compelled me to stay longer than I intended and prodded me as a trained therapeutic interviewer later in my career, to ask questions that led to more questions. Enthralled as I was during visits to their shops and in some cases the graciousness of their homes, the final result is the book you, the reader, have in your hands.

However, as you will soon discover, works this distinctive and often precious are often imbued with the former owner's energy or even followed by the original owner themselves: the kind of owner who no longer breathes, no longer drinks or shares dinner with their family or friends. Having passed away, their homes were probably sold or auctioned. For most, the material objects that punctuated their lives stay behind, in a dusty cupboard, in a living room of a descendant, or are part of a vendor's sale. For some of the objects, the deceased owner somehow felt an indelible attachment to the piece of craftsmanship or work of art or both. When that happens, whoever desires to become the next owner faces a challenge.

The first narrative is my own foray into the unknown in the form of a beautiful, brocaded Queen Anne chair. The next four are from respected small antique dealers and their shops. I thank each and every one of them for sharing their experiences with me as a fellow antique aficionado. Though I changed names and kept the locations obscure for their sakes, the narrative comes straight from their hearts. I hope you enjoy this book as much as I have enjoyed writing it.

Anna Maria Manalo
March 16, 2022
Lacoste, France

PART I

THE QUEEN ANNE WING CHAIR

CHAPTER 1

While living in Connecticut, I often visited and browsed through several estate sales, flea markets and antique shops of higher vintage. Parts of Connecticut as well as Rhode Island, Massachusetts, Vermont and Maine, which I had the opportunity to visit, are replete with fine antiques. By virtue of their history in the formation of the first American colonies, these areas are treasure troves but also, by geography, had their share of fine and rare objects from Europe.

I was always open to the unusual as well as objects made overseas in far-off Europe and Asia, the latter continent where I was born and raised. How these distinctive and valued possessions came to be in the hands of the current seller always intrigued me. Sadly, during that time of my salad days, I often subsisted on dormitory meals, as they were included in my tuition, and worked part-time as a per diem at the local mental health hospital in order to gain some semblance of income. This employment at the same time allowed me to garner experience and insight, as psychology was my major.

Freed a bit from financial restrictions, I would join my room-mate and friends for that occasional hop on the train to New York City, which was a mere thirty-minute train ride on the Metro-North. The city proved to be a mecca of antiques as well, but these visits were fruitless, as they were out of my financial league. That being the case, I confined my antique searches, a world before the internet, to local shops and flea markets in the small but picturesque towns of Connecticut and nearby New England states. Today, it would not have mattered, as Connecticut now has a lifestyle that commands a high-end bracket of income.

Despite the limitations of my funds, I remained undeterred from traipsing through vintage and flea market antiques, some questionable in origin and kept "close to the vest" of the unknown seller. My interest in these found objects spurned a desire to observe, learn and, finally, plan to someday acquire some of these fine collections.

At that time, antiques of interest to me included furniture, which proved even dearer, or as the French would say, *plus cher*. Meanwhile, I learned all I could and, in so doing, found myself separating from my group of friends to take the lonely bus or train to not-so-often visited spots where these markets and shops were located: away from clubs, pubs and clothes shop-ping. Dusty, cluttered, musty and dark places were often the type of shops I entered lest they be the open air of a summer outdoor market, which I found more pleasing, but not often.

On one of these outdoor flea market forages with the companionship of a friend with a vehicle, we wandered into one of the seaside towns of picture-postcard Connecticut on a raw and blustery fall day. Upon arrival at the open festival of sorts, we wove through and perused one outdoor spread of vintage objects after another. Hours later, I stumbled upon a cushioned chair that appeared to be a Queen Anne in style, softly but firmly padded in brocade fabric with cherry wood legs and wings on both sides of the seatback. I queried the silent vendor, who offered for me to sit on the article of furniture. It appeared to be in sound condition. I quickly surmised that the piece of furniture, brocaded in an ashes of roses pink with a spray of small flowers, was out of my funding league. Until I asked.

I was astounded to find that the chair in fact was only thirty-five dollars. I swiftly dug into my shoulder bag, a leather affair purchased at another flea market in a borough of Brooklyn. Having handed the paltry sum saved over from my per diem job at the hospital, the seller's frown turned to a semblance of a grin. I, of course, in my late teens did not query, out of eagerness, about the history of said object/furniture. Nor did I care at the time its actual value or true vintage, as "beggars can't be choosers," as the saying goes. It was sturdy, appeared moth-free as I recall, and had a very comfortable seat considering its supposed advertised age. I doubt that the vendor, a withered man of indeterminate age who was huddled in the back of a pockmarked flatbed truck (reeking of cigars), would volunteer or know the origins of my object of joy. I picked up the chair, which stank of the man's cigars on closer inspection, and a male friend proceeded to haul it into the back of his Beetle convertible, happy to move on to the next and more interesting destination: a beer pub for lunch.

It was not until I got back to the dormitory, an all-women's haven of English majors, art and history buffs, and a sordid group of strait-laced premeds, that I discovered the chair came with an occupant. So begins my story.

Now duly blessed with me as the proud owner, the chair sat in the corner by the sole window of my private dorm room. I plunked a white lace pillow I'd inherited from my mother's boudoir onto the sturdy seat back, ready and waiting for a visitor – right next to my dorm room desk and a swivel chair I'd salvaged from a retiring professor. A welcome addition, I thought, as it served as an additional seat for visiting friends and family other than my desk chair and bed. It made the room cozy and lent an aura of sophistication in a room that was outfitted identically to all the others on that dorm floor. It felt distinctive and made me feel sophisticated, particularly feeling that it was a "steal." In retrospect, I think it was me who was stolen from.

I sprayed it with a can of Lysol on the first evening, not realizing what that simple act of disinfecting would dredge up – or perhaps it was the change in location to a Jesuit university replete with nuns who rented the next wing. I don't know to this day. So as I blessed it with Lysol, the room took on a less musty smell, and the foul odor of cigars was obliterated.

Allow me to digress a bit about where my dormitory was: at the edge of the small private college I attended sits the all-women's dormitory, Saint Justina Hall, which was where I was living for two semesters. It was a building usually requested by coeds who crave the privacy of a single room in order to study in silence, to create works of art or to write. I found myself in my second year at the university for all those reasons, particularly when the rest of the campus seemed avid to attend celebrations of every kind, with beer flowing like a stream and, at times, a river. I moved there to gain some semblance of sanity after finding the beer-swilling freshmen who punctuated the halls of the coed dorm every weekend where I was annoying and unproductive. The ensuing vomitus in the common bathrooms proved too much for me.

I was on the top floor of this three-story stone building built around the nineteenth century. On this floor there were about twenty single rooms and a large common bathroom equipped with shower stalls and toilets. My room was at the very end of the wing, at the extreme opposite of the wing that was rented at the time by nuns of the Dominican order, habit-less but chaste by habit. Thus, by virtue of its location at the edge of the campus where two sides faced a forest and one a quiet neighborhood of older stately homes (old money) the dormitory was very quiet, assuring us of privacy and deep study.

CHAPTER 2

The first evening after my acquisition of said chair found me arriving back early from the cafeteria after an early dinner. My plan was to eat early so I could get a head start on reviewing for finals, which was the following week. It was about two weeks before the end of the first semester, which in American universities at the time meant there was a monthlong winter break that we were collectively looking forward to after a very demanding semester.

I had just been asked by the head of the English department to consider switching my major to English, with Creative Writing in mind. For lack of better foresight, I turned it down, as I was bent on pursuing a degree where I could practice as a therapist of sorts as a clinician. It was primarily why I moonlighted on weekends as a mental health worker at the nearby mental facility, I told the elegant lady, a full professor in tweeds.

I recall enjoying the locked ward, listening to the soft music meant to lull the manic and anxious and put into soporific stupor the depressed. I recall the display of half-smoked cigarettes in ashtrays and the chronically sharpened pencils, which was a subtle demand for us, the staff, to chronicle observations in the treatment plants and reports of every shift. "EMA" for early morning awakening, red dots for "watch," yellow for "non-compliant" and so on and so on. DSM-3, the Diagnostic Standard of Mental Disorders, Axis one, two, three, four and five. A book we were learning by heart as part of our part-time job. It was not good at the change of shifts to hear someone had "escalated" and "four-point restraints" were used. That meant that if they were still restrained in bed by the time our shift began at three p.m., we had to take a turn every fifteen minutes to do a bed check. Even more so on a suicide attempt. Those watches felt endless. After I acquired the chair, that watch was a delight, or any watch for that matter, as I began dreading going back to my dorm room where the chair sat.

On this particular evening, the day of classes completed, I was set with books, writing utensils, highlighters of every color, and notecards to commence reviewing for exams. From the cafeteria, it was a ten-minute walk to the dormitory or a quick two-minute hop on the free shuttle bus. I picked the latter, as the shuttle bus sat, engine idling, as I exited the back end of the cafeteria. Right on time for me to just hop in and enjoy the falling leaves gracing the grass as it wound its brief travel up the winding slope to the hill that held the stone walls of Saint Justina Hall. Out of the growing chill and shortened days, I looked forward to a hot cup of chocolate, marshmallows, and a heady review of inorganic chemistry. Yech.

As soon as the dormitory building appeared, the portico visible from my seat, I saw three girls, including the floor's room advisor, standing and appearing to be waiting for me. Surely, not me, I thought. As the small bus approached, they saw me seated towards the front of the bus and huddled closer to the curb against the frigid breeze of approaching night, pointedly looking straight at me. The first idea that came to mind was that my mother, my aunt or my uncle was sick or had some accident.

Needless to say, I bolted out of the bus as soon as it stopped under the portico, as I was the sole passenger.

~

So HERE'S the story from the advisor, an upperclassman from Long Island.

My dorm mate, Jane, a buxom young blonde from down the hall, had knocked on my door. She apparently was hunting for some creamer for her coffee. (We were allowed a small refrigerator, microwave and coffee or teapot in our rooms for convenience.) Noting my door was mysteriously ajar, which I never do, as I am security-conscious and was raised in a security-conscious household, she took it upon herself to allow herself in.

Behold.

There was a "young woman with a fedora hat" there, she said. According to Jane, the woman "looked upset" and seemed "glassine." Glassine? That's when she realized that perhaps she was looking at someone who wasn't breathing. The woman just stared back at her in silence. Sitting, the woman was, legs crossed in a flouncy bluish-whitish dress, she told the dorm resident advisor. High heels, long gloves, etc. In short, clad in some outfit as if she were waiting for a hansom cab on her way to the opera.

What the heck? Come on. Are you expecting your sister? the advisor asked. I don't have one. AND why would she dress that way? I queried. Did anyone let her in? This latter question the advisor asked of the other two girls. Don't know. Your door was unlocked; she turned back to me. I hardly leave it unlocked unless I'm just visiting down the hall or in the shower. Two other dorm mates, one new this semester (What was her name again?) and a friend of a friend who usually used the piano room at the other end near the nuns stood there gawking.

Emmie. She looked frightened like sardines on white toast, tiny fish eyes staring back in shock.

Finally, the group parted, and I walked in out of the cold, and the retinue followed me up the elevator. I wondered if someone played with my lock and stole something from my room. Why my room? Why would she be so dressed up like she was PART of an opera? Plus Denise, my next-door neighbor, is extremely nosy. She would have heard if she was home studying, which is what she usually does, eating late at the cafeteria after all the homework, papers, etc. were done. Maybe that guy who dresses in drag for fun whom she had been dating was playing a prank? The exchange student from Germany. Everbrut, or something like that.

As the elevator whooshed open, we all exited at the same time, a feat never done before. I had to squeeze past Emmie-whatever in her Bass shoes and eternal L.L.Bean Fair Isle sweater. Right in front of me sat Jane in a cheap short robe, slippers and shorts, white as Tupperware plastic in the glare of the fluorescent light that lit the elevator banks. There WAS someone in your room, Elise! (My middle name is Elisa, and friends call me Elise as they brutalize Elisa to Eloise, Elsa and some unspeakable configuration.) I ignored Jane, who was still wearing terry shorts under the revealing robe and her eternally damp hair despite the growing chill of late fall.

I marched with the retinue behind me, now with Jane added to the group. I felt the breath of the room advisor right by my shoulder as she breathed through her mouth: a very irritating habit, which left me wondering if she was asthmatic like me as a child.

We arrived at the end of the hall, where my door stood wide open, the window in my room somehow ajar and wide open as well. Papers were strewn all over the floor and some plastered on the walls as the wind and leaves blew in. It was cold. VERY cold.

She was sitting right there, pointed Jane, her teeth clicking like she was wearing false teeth. Jane was actually SCARED, which was so unlike the girl I knew who played soccer and hiked the Adirondacks.

The advisor strode past me and into the room, as if she was on a mission to rectify the situation. She pulled the window shut, lever down, drew the curtains and turned to me. You need to make sure the window is shut before you leave. With the door open, the entire dorm will freeze. It's flu season. No, really. I wasn't going to argue. I always kept it shut with the lever down and the door locked. Okay, she said. I've seen worse, but I hope you can get your term papers back in order, or you'll be typing them all over again. Yup.

I began collecting the papers, and the friend of a friend stayed back to help me collect the precious pieces. It was before laptops and cell mobiles. Jane stood in the hall, unsure what to do next, until the room advisor ushered her back down the hall to her room. I'll report the incident to security, okay? I heard parts of Jane's conversation, which went in the vein of "But the woman was very strange…"

The friend of the friend, plus Marcie from Bridgeport, stacked the rest of my term paper on top of my presswood dresser and said she had to go back to campus and get dinner. Thanks for your help, I said. I think she already ate dinner and was just looking for an excuse to get the heck away from whatever was in my room. Emmie waved goodbye in silence, and her Bass shoes clicked down the hall, away from my strange room.

Alone in the room, I knocked on the wall to rouse my next-door neighbor. Of course if she had been in, she would have come out and joined us by now. No one home, as I expected. I turned up the thermostat by the front door, switched on a few lamps by my desk, and turned my back on the CHAIR to switch on my coffee maker to heat some water for chocolate. I turned back around, expecting a woman to be there. No fedora, no glas-sine lady. Just a brocade-covered chair. She must've been smoking reefer, this Jane. Good.

By eleven, I was done reviewing for the night. A timid tap on my door. Denise. We popped some popcorn in her air popper next door and called it a night after the late news on her little set. I slept dreaming Jane came back with the lady with the high heels and fedora hat. The lady was wearing Jane's terry shorts, and her hair was wet like Jane's.

CHAPTER 3

The end of the week found me contemplating a trip by train to New York. It was a plan hatched by a few friends who wanted to see a play, which back then was not as expensive as it is today, but still not as cheap as I liked. On this occasion, we collectively picked an off-Broadway production (for the life of me I cannot recall the production nor the cast), which actually ended up being in Brooklyn. The room advisor, keen on keeping her job, remained unduly conscientious and paid a visit to my dorm room to check that it was locked. It was, Denise told me later.

Off we went into Manhattan for lunch and then the play at 4 p.m., just in time for a late dinner later back on campus. I think I was so excited at the time I forgot I told my friend Sherry from another dorm that if she couldn't find her crib notes for the Art History exam (we both took it as an elective), she could knock on Denise's door next to me, and she would let her in. We had keys to each other's rooms just in case of a fire, but no one else had my key but Denise.

At the duly appointed hour of library study, Sherry, like clockwork, walked down to Saint "J" and knocked on Denise's door. Out came Denise, my spare key in hand, and unlocked my door.

Before Sherry could turn on the light, she smelled perfume. Like an overpowering scent enough to make her think someone WAS in my room. Remember I'd sprayed Lysol all over the chair to dispel any scent. "It" was back. The strangeness. And, no, I did not take my mother's L'Air du Temps perfume with me. Denise turned on the light and began fanning the room with her hands. It was a cloying scent. Unpleasantly strong, they recounted.

Then they both saw smoke coming from the corner of the room where the chair sat. Both she and Sherry smelled it. Like a chemistry class. Denise, disgusted, thought I had taken up a habit. What odor was I trying to mask? That could cause a fire, the room advisor said later. Denise searched the corner behind the chair, the room, looked in the trash bin, and couldn't locate why smoke was coming out of the corner.

Until she looked right at the chair.

The chair was smoking.

Denise grabbed my coffee mug, filled it with tap water and approached, examining it, ready to douse it and destroy the fabric. Sherry touched the chair, assuming it would be hot to the touch. It wasn't.

The smoke suddenly disappeared.

Then the window blew open.

I came back to the dorm to find another group of students waiting for me. This time, the advisor was upset.

Two days later, a student, Gina, exited her room just two doors down and saw the same hatted lady in heels. It came out of my room and FLOATED, yes, FLOATED towards her. She screamed, and that had everyone running out of their rooms to look. My door was locked, and no sign of the supposed lady. I became famous overnight because of my room. I was holding hostage a woman in distress, wearing outdated clothes.

The weekend of the NEXT encounter found me at the hospital, dreading what might happen next, as it seemed that these episodes happened when I wasn't in the room. I was in suspense during the entire shift. I had begun dreading what was happening in my room and what I'd brought home with the chair.

I'd kept vigil one night, sitting on my bed with a book open, one eye on the chair. Nothing. Back then, I was not into the supernatural and still remembered the incidents in the haunted home across the street in the neighborhood where I grew up. A haunted neighborhood, as a matter of fact, a medley of Japanese soldiers buried all over the neighborhood, under the houses. That story was told in detail in my first book, *Portal*. I didn't need THAT following me here – a respite from all that chaos and fear now that I was living halfway around the globe. Now this.

Truly, the incidents with my dorm mates and friend Sherry made the chair less attractive to me. I sought to look for a place to trash the chair if the events continued. The luster of its vintage or supposed vintage status began to ebb like a Volvo with no spare parts.

The shift at the hospital was uneventful and rather dull. I passed the key to the ward to people on the next shift, advising them on the notations of the meds that had all been given out by the duty nurse without incident. Then I drove back through the quiet roads through town and snaked down the narrow road towards Saint Justina Hall at the edge of the campus. The parking lot next to the dorm was quiet, as expected, being a late Sunday night. The next day, Monday, was the last day for reviews, at least for me and some of my dorm mates. Then midterms were upon us.

CHAPTER 4

I looked up at my window and noted the dim light, which would be the nightlight I left on. The next window over was Denise next door, lights still blazing. Half my neighbors in my hall were up, and the faint sound of violin music and an assortment of Springsteen and Billy Joel could be heard through their windows. Good. A very normal, average night before a new week. Elitists and preppies and mysterious Latino Asians like me mixed in one building.

The elevator whooshed open, and the music from different rooms all blended together, as some dorm rooms were open. However, as I approached the end of my wing, it became quieter, more subdued, like an odd duck in a lake of geese. The more studious end of the wing. I passed Denise's door and stood to unlock mine, a photo of my New York group of friends who trained into Brooklyn with me for a play pinned to the door. I took it down, noting it came with a note from Dave, my erstwhile flea market buddy who had hauled the "chair of suspicious origins" in his Beetle. The photo of the group stared back at me as if accusatory. As I plucked it off and entered, tossing my coat on the bed, I noted the room was warm and toasty. I'll get back to Dave later and his note.

I proceeded to riffle through my books to prepare to hunker down for the night, my stack of ready notes outlined on four-by-six-inch note cards. Concept names with a sentence or two on the back to jog my memory, and then shuffle them to help recall out of order. This should be fun, as I liked abnormal psychology. In my wheelhouse, as my professor would say, while he touched his handlebar mustache and drummed his growing paunch. Thus absorbed with the minutiae of study, I forgot about Dave's note and settled into my swivel chair.

The chair squeaked as the night wore on, screaming to be oiled and my back yelling for a change of position. So I stood, forgetting I had neglected to get water for the hot chocolate I would later need during my break. I had decided that if Denise was timing her study break, which she often did, the unspoken rule was to take it by midnight. I grabbed the pot from its corner by the hot plate and darted out into the hall for the water cooler. Having filled the pot for at least two people, I took my time walking back down to my end of the hall, noting in my slippered feet how silent the dorm had become.

I reentered minutes later to observe that the room had remarkably cooled, so much so that now I felt I needed the hot chocolate sooner than I thought. I turned on the portable electric stove with its two heating elements and plunked down the pot, now filled with at least four mugs of hot water.

I sat back down on the squeaky chair and thought it squeaked my name: Elise. Ignoring it, I proceeded with my review. Minutes of silence ensued.

The kettle began whistling, awakening me from my concentration. Two mugs, which contained hot chocolate powder from Swiss Miss, sat from the previous night when I had originally intended to brew. I inspected one mug for ants, convinced it was still good. I poured the steaming water, hoping the scent wouldn't carry into the hall, inviting an eternal friend, Bernice, who loved food breaks. Sipping, with the hot steam fogging my glasses, I sat on the swivel chair and saw that I had dropped Dave's note to the floor under the CHAIR.

I placed the mug on the desk, leaned over to grab the note.

A sigh.

I paused, pulled away and sat back, looking around.

Then I felt a breath near my left ear.

The chair.

I was perplexed, then felt sadness.

Then I felt the hairs on my arms go up.

I shot up from my seat.

A strong sense of foreboding filled my psyche.

Someone was in my room.

I moved away, turned and bolted from the room.

Out the door and into the hallway.

Denise emerged from her room next door.

"What's the matter?"

"You won't..." My face must have been a mask of fear.

"The chair..."

"How did you guess?" I asked sarcastically as I turned back.

Denise flew past me and stood at the threshold of my room. "What did you see?"

I sighed, and the simple act reminded me of what I'd just heard.

I heard another intake of breath and leaped.

Emmie was looking over my shoulder.

"Please. Don't do that again!"

Denise entered the room; I followed, Emmie at my heels.

She picked up the folded note under the chair, handed it to me.

It was in Dave's precise handwriting, a would-be architect's penmanship: ELISE – CALL ME. IT'S ABOUT THE CHAIR.

CHAPTER 5

I awakened on Denise's floor, the quilt wrapped around my pajamas like a cocoon. Underneath, I felt the squish of plastic and remembered I was lying on the floor, with Denise's sleeping bag insulating me from the cold parquet floor. I looked up and saw the fringe of Denise's comforter lined precisely as she had made her bed prior to leaving.

Bolting up after seeing the sunlight, I realized I was running late for breakfast and, thus, the first midterm. In trepidation, I reentered my unlocked door, recalling the scare of the previous night and my reluctance to sleep there. I paused by the closet, surveying the small room, my eyes landing on the chair. The sun was streaming from the window, lighting the brocade fabric and reflecting the gold thread. The chair looked cheerful in the daylight, as I'd seen it the first time when it sat outdoors at the flea market. Nearby, my bed still held my fresh clothes, which I had laid out prior to bedding down on Denise's floor the night before. The room felt different with the glow of the sun to dispel what might lie unseen. Relaxing, I quickly changed and ran down the steps, hoping the shuttle bus was at the portico.

Of course, it wasn't.

I ran down the lane, my messenger back thumping by my side, my slim volume of review notebooks with me. No point in taking books along, as whatever didn't make it to my memory would not be there in the remaining minutes before the two major exams.

As I sat in the amphitheater, waiting for the midterm to be handed out, I observed two of the girls from the dorm talking below me towards the front. I looked down at my pencils, not wishing to make eye contact, as the dreadful episodes with my new piece of furniture had by now circulated past my floor of the dorm. I wanted to focus on my exam at hand and didn't want to deal with the gossip the chair had unwittingly initiated.

A middle-aged Jesuit priest dressed in clerical collar trudged up the aisle, handing out copies of the exam. Since I usually sat high up and on an aisle seat, this class was no exception, so he would be handing me the sheaf of papers and the small blue notebooks we were expected to fill in response to five essay questions.

The professor, a man also in his late forties, was passing the blue notebooks, following behind the clergyman. As the priest approached, he paused, making eye contact with me. I recognized him from the ministry, and his office was at the rectory adjacent to the chapel. He was obviously assisting on this day and appeared to recognize me, though I could not recall his name. He stopped by my chair, handed me the exam copies while he studied me, and asked me to take one and pass the rest to the row to my right. Fine. The comfort of routine.

Then he seemed to be deep in thought, grappling with an internal question that seemed close to his lips.

I sensed it was important to him.

"Do you need help?"

I glanced back, unsure of his meaning.

"You brought something to the dorm recently."

Our eyes locked.

"Oh, that."

"Yes, that."

I looked around, conscious of my seatmate.

"I can come and bless it if you're willing. I strongly recommend it."

I nodded.

He gave me the semblance of a smile. "I'll call and ask for you, and we can make an appointment."

"Thank you, Father."

"The sooner the better."

"Yes, Father."

He patted me on the shoulder and resumed handing out the exams.

I looked forward and caught the eyes of the two girls below me from the dorm. They quickly turned away and faced front.

I leaned into the first page of the test.

My hands were shaking as I scribbled my name on the test.

CHAPTER 6

Marcie bolted down the hall towards me, the soles of her rabbit slippers making a clack, clack, clack sound on the linoleum. I had just exited the elevator and returned from an early dinner.

She pointed at the phone banks past the common bathrooms. "There's a guy named Dave on the phone."

I hadn't planned on calling him until the end of the week after midterms were done. It was unlike him. I wondered why it couldn't wait.

I picked up the hall phone.

"You still have that chair in your room?"

"Umm... yeah."

An intake of breath. "Get rid of it."

"I'm getting it blessed, if that's what you mean."

"Get rid of it. Totally."

I looked around, checking to make sure no one was within earshot. Of course, Jane's door was open. I put the phone down, the cord dangling. I peered into the room, past the closet. She must be in the bathroom.

"Dave, can I come to you? It's more private."

"Sure. After dinner around sevenish?"

I looked at my watch. It was 5:30. "I guess this can't wait."

"I'd rather not."

"Okay."

"Be here. I am going to reserve the study room on my floor so we can talk."

"I'll knock on your door."

"Cool. Bring your books if you need to."

"Can I stay over?"

A pause. Oh, shit. "No, silly. I don't mean it that way."

Dave chuckles. "Yeah, okay. I gotcha. Didn't think so, but you never know." A pause. "Elise?"

"Yeah?"

"It's bad, isn't it? On your end?"

"I'll tell you when I see you."

"You gotta sell it or toss it. I'm telling you."

That weekend, I had another shift at the hospital. Overnight. Glad for it, as I needn't find a place to sleep.

CHAPTER 7

Father Neumann's dorm was coed. Dave's wing was on the right of the quadrangle, a brick building with five floors. All men. In the center was a series of four study rooms, which students who needed quiet on the weeknights could reserve ahead for study in groups or individually if needed. The left wing was all girls.

I had my duvet and books with me, a toothbrush and change of clothes. It made it look like Dave and I were into something heavy, as it was a midterm week when most people only had studying in mind. However, I didn't care. I didn't want to over-stay my welcome with my neighbor Denise, and Bernice, who would have kept me up all night with her television and eternal bag of popcorn, wasn't on my option list.

I could've gone to the beach houses and stayed with my art friends Trey and Lucas, but I didn't even dawn on me it would get this far. I made a note to call them and perhaps visit to let them know my situation. I truly hated to impose, but theirs would be ideal, as it was an entire beach house. What would be a better excuse? The shuttle would take me there for free – a mere five miles down the road, facing the Atlantic.

I stepped up to the front door, and a young man, a senior, held the door for me. He winked, and I gave a semblance of a grin. I wondered what he was thinking, with my change of clothes and the duvet over my shoulder. Oh well. Shit happens. The priest hadn't called, and I made a mental note to pay a visit to the ministry office to see if I could discuss what he knew about the chair and the goings-on since it had come into my possession.

Suddenly, I had a lot to do besides study and work at the hospital. I needed to unload the chair. It was truly now a pain in my...

Dave was his usual self, except I detected he needed sleep. His two roommates were both in, hanging out huddled with a can of beer each and a hot bowl of popcorn. They appeared ensconced for the night with a movie, and one extended his hand and offered me a beer. Wilt or Winston or something. He had deep blue eyes and a shock of blond hair. Taken, I was sure. I thanked him, but declined the offer, as I needed a clear head for a good review of my Renaissance Art elective. With his books under his arm, Dave led the way into the study room with its view of the quadrangle and the students moving to and fro under the streetlights. It was a frosty night.

"You look like you've been burning the midnight oil."

Dave looked at me askance. "I wish it were from studying for the exams, but it's not."

I looked back, concerned, guilty, even scolded.

Dave leaned back on the armchair after shutting the door, a leather affair, outdated but comfortable. I pulled my knees up, studying him, waiting.

He twirled his pen. "Let's say I have not had a good night's sleep since I brought back that chair for you." He peered at me from his Coke-bottle glasses. A bit like John Lennon without the goatee.

"I'm listening."

"I don't know about you, but the first night back..."

"Yeah..."

"The first night back? I had a nightmare of sorts... well, a lot of nightmares."

I put my feet down and moved the chair closer. "I feel bad I brought this on you. I truly..."

"I saw a woman... hat like in the '20s. Stiletto heels or something like that old-fashioned stuff from the roaring..."

I finished for him: "Twenties. Bluish dress..."

"Yup. You saw her too?" I now had his full attention.

"No, but Jane did. Then another girl... then..." I told him everything.

"Well, it's strange. Here, you know... guys go gaga when they see a woman in the showers. Someone saw her or thought they saw a woman following ME into the shower!"

"Tell me again."

"Hat like the ones they used in the olden days... bluish white dress... she was kinda shimmering... this is all in a nightmare... three nights in a row. Then the night before... you know Ed?"

"The resident priest?"

"Yup. He was the one who saw her follow me into the bathroom."

"Great."

He was nodding with gravity. "Get rid of it. I thought at first I just ate too much at night. Priests don't take that lightly."

"I'm having it blessed, Dave."

"I told you. It won't work. This thing's got a bad vibe."

"Trust me. It will. Only a ghost... unlike my old neighborhood."

Dave shakes his head.

He nervously taps the table.

He looks away in disagreement. "I need my sleep. So do you."

"Just let me get it blessed..."

"If it doesn't work, will you let me take it out and toss it?"

"As in a dumpster?"

"As in a dump site. Somewhere across state lines..." Dave was serious.

"Deal. Let's hear what Joy has to say."

Joy was Joy Bernard, a classmate living in the same dorm as Dave, who was reputedly psychic and worked with tarot cards and did seances. Lately, she had been hanging out with us plus her friend Karin. We were the fringe group. Totally.

"Okay. Get it blessed, consult Joy, and then we trash it if it doesn't work." This time Dave looked straight at me.

CHAPTER 8

Father McMillan was prompt. Right on the minute, he stood outside my door at seven p.m. Denise, Emmie, the room advisor, Jean and myself were in the room. He was dressed in what I called "priestly garb" at the time: a purple stole, a white gown and black shoes, as far as I can remember. He had a Bible with him, a large crucifix and a large vial of holy water, which he opened once I let him in. He also had a relic of a saint, I forget which one. He had actually been a priest for some time by the time he joined the campus ministry and used to teach at another college in the Midwest. This I learned after the blessing, an affair that seemed brief and to the point.

What I do remember is how the room seemed to warm up without the thermostat being jacked up. He intoned prayer after prayer, asking us to join in, and the chanting made the room cheerier, hopeful and warm. I know it wasn't my imagination. I do remember that. I remember being hopeful that the beautiful chair was mine forever until I moved it to my very own house. I remember the scent of burning leaves outside even though the window was closed. I remembered the scent of a candle taking over the room, borrowed from Emmie, who loved candles. It conjured visions of Christmas as if it were holly berry.

He walked out, contented that whatever came with the chair had left us in peace. After all, in two weeks, it would be Christmas.

I called Dave from the hall phone as soon as the rite was over, telling him how it went and how relieved I was. He said, "Elise, give it a week or two. We'll be gone for the Christmas break, and hopefully we'll come back to a peaceful room, and you and I can sleep."

But less than two days had gone by when the next event happened.

I remember it was a Wednesday since midterms were over.

CHAPTER 9

Dave wanted the chair out. I guess because his intentions were strong, he ended up being left alone, his nights full of study and deep, relaxed sleep. On my end, I held on to the wish that I could keep the chair, a bargain considering how it looked and felt when I sat on it. I felt expensive, classy, even important. I found out shortly that my desire to own it didn't sit well with the previous owner.

Then the blessing.

On the third night after the blessing, I woke up to screaming right outside my window. Lights came on, the hall lights flooded under the doors, and the room advisor came padding down the hall, checking everyone.

Voices from the rooms, doors opening; slippers flooded the hallway. I emerged into chaos, still partly asleep after several nights of worry and restless study.

A woman in her forties and a nun dressed in headgear and civilian clothes were busy explaining to the room advisor, who appeared very troubled. They proceeded to enter Bernice's dorm room, and I wrapped my robe around me and followed a few of the girls, including Denise and Emmie, to Bernice's room. I felt like a gawker, one of those people you see who watch a car accident minutes before the ambulance arrives. But Bernice was a friend of sorts, and we wondered what had happened at two a.m. that involved her.

Bernice was actually standing outside her door, appearing to be flabbergasted and obviously awakened from sleep. Her room's window was over the portico, and three women – the nun, the advisor and another woman whom I didn't know – were all crowded around the window: they were watching whatever was transpiring on the ground below by the portico.

"You okay?" I asked Bernice.

"She's fine," Emmie replied on Bernice's behalf.

"They knocked on my door after the screams. I just figured I'd move out of the way," Bernice replied. So she wasn't involved.

I walked in as soon as the nun and the room advisor walked away from the window and hurried down to the elevators, their middle-aged shoes padding down the hall. Whatever was happening was outside, as I thought. The woman stranger was a resident artist and introduced herself. She walked away and marched towards the elevator banks to join the other two women.

Through the window we looked. A nun was outside in a jogging outfit, one of her sneakers off as if she had fallen. Was she mugged? It was not that type of neighborhood, but there's always a first time, I thought. Then an ambulance came. Two technicians approached the nun, their bags opened. They appeared to be bandaging a leg. Eventually, the woman stood, limped and was ushered into the back of the ambulance. Behind us, the room advisor had returned. She briskly clapped her hands like a schoolteacher to a bunch of schoolkids, prodding us to return to our rooms.

"Someone must've hit her on the leg."

"She got mugged."

"A nun. Imagine that."

"She was just jogging."

And so on and so on. I shut the door, turned up the heat, and slipped promptly into oblivion.

In the cafeteria, I carried my tray of eggs, premade hash browns, and a bowl of Cheerios sans milk and approached the customary table of suspects, my New York friends. Among them sat Dave, all huddled together. Denise sat near the center of the long table and looked up first as I approached.

They all stopped and looked up at me as I plopped my tray down and sat.

Bernice, not normally a table member, was there too. She spoke first. "The nun? She met up with your lady of the infamous chair – with hat and heels."

Dave appeared terrified behind his Coke-bottle glasses. Denise nodded grimly in agreement. She looked piqued. Almost sordid.

"How did you guys find out?" I ventured.

Apparently, Marcie had been listening to the room advisor talk to the nun. The nun was jogging back down towards our building, and there was a woman there, all dressed like Marcie saw... same description.

"What happened to the nun?"

"She saw the woman, thought she was kinda odd... jogged past her, then before you know it, the woman's eyes were blazing as the nun jogged by." Denise swallowed, warming to her story.

Then Marcie interjected: "The same woman I saw exit your room. She was downright glaring at the nun, so the nun did a double take and got really scared. The woman ran after her, but she saw the woman was..."

"Floating," Denise finished.

Marcie nodded, her face stunned.

Snickers from the group. But Marcie and Denise weren't laughing.

"Then before she knew it, the slap on her leg, and she fell."

"What happened to the woman who was floating?" This was Dave.

"She disappeared," Bernice interjected.

Nervous laughter.

Another tray plopped at the end of the table. It was Joy Bernard. "I got an idea."

Dave interrupted: "This isn't a game, Joy."

"I'm not treating it like a game," Joy said defensively.

"Guys... " Denise, the self-proclaimed referee.

"Just listen..." Joy offered.

"Okay. What do you suggest?" I ventured again.

Let's toss it, one said. Yup. Okay, where? Town dump is where it's headed, another said. No, get Father McMillan again, another said. I told them I had tried the blessing, and I was willing and open to suggestions. Dave raised his hand.

"Yes, Dave?"

"Let's allow the priest another chance. Okay, Elise?"

"Yes. I feel like we need to leave this up to the ministry," I agreed.

"But the priest may not be available for another week." This from Bernice.

"Joy?" Denise ventured. Dave rolled his eyes.

Joy was ready: "I got a plan while you arrange with Father McMillan. First, you need to move the chair out of the dorm, as SHE doesn't like it there."

CHAPTER 10

Dave single-handedly hauled the chair and sat on it as he descended the elevator. I followed, jumped in, and off we went.

Downstairs, Marcie, Denise and I uneventfully hauled it onto his Beetle, then the short trip to the beach house where our friends Trey and Lucas lived facing a local beach. At the time, we thought a rental was the ideal place where Joy Bernard could do what she felt might work to get rid of the "occupant" of the chair. In deference to them and in my own selfish stubbornness to hold on to the chair, I agreed for a seance to be conducted by our self-proclaimed psychic friend. Call us sophomoric, childish, dramatic, you choose, but it seemed to make sense while we waited for the ministry and was a measure to get the chair off-campus and the university out of our hair. Little did we know what could result from such an act. Not one of us was even of the legal drinking age of the day, though it was eighteen at the time. Our decisions were based on a bunch of sophomores looking for some excitement. I believe now, several years later as a much wiser and better-informed adult, that staging a seance was downright foolish, if not dangerous in retrospect.

Early December sent gales of laughing wind, mocking us collectively in our foolish attempt to rid the chair of the occupant. Connecticut in the early 1980s, way before we even had any awareness of global warming, exuded its typical New England landscape: a bending wind, a beach strewn with white wafting water and rolling waves on a gray landscape. The beach house, one of several, faced the Atlantic less than thirty yards from the surf. The mood presented an appropriate nor'easter for what we were about to do. The front of the rental house, meant for beachgoers, was a double glassed-in porch of sorts, windows shut this time of year. Brown cedar shingle siding, which is typical of the area, wrapped the humble house from the elements.

With the advent of winter, Trey and Lucas had sealed the porch windows in plastic to reduce the drafts that might invade the front living area and kitchen, which housed a stone fireplace and cold wooden floors. The plastic was such that whatever view of the ocean was there during the summer months was obliterated by the translucent covering, more functional than aesthetic to help with the heating bills of two college students.

Joy positioned THE chair by the wide fireplace, the logs now crackling with tendrils of a growing fire, as if someone were going to sit and read us some campfire stories. She asked us to sit a few feet away at a round wooden dining table positioned in the center of the room. It was pockmarked with the remains of a pizza from last night's Friday dinner. Lucas cleared the debris, wiping it off with an old tee shirt from an eponymous guitar concert.

The eight of us sat: Dave to my right, Trey to my left. Joy had the chair behind her, closest to her in proximity, with her back to the fireplace. Dave's two roommates, there out of curiosity, sat to either side of Joy, with Lucas and Bernice making up the rest of the table.

Armed with a large candle with three wicks and salt sans crystal ball, Joy plopped the candle on a small plate provided by Lucas on the fireplace hearth and made a circle of salt around it. Then she lit it.

"Don't you want it on the table?" Trey asked.

"No, but this will be..." With a flourish, Joy unfolded a Ouija board, tatty and dusty, the kind you see from Hasbro. She took a small shot glass and placed it on the center fold of the board – and told us to put one finger on it. We all reached, curious, as we'd never participated before. Confident she had done this for quite some time (we never asked), we awaited further instructions.

Joy leaned back, shut her eyes, and then asked Trey to turn all the lights off. Dave protested. Denise asked if we could at least keep one light on. Joy acquiesced, and Trey left on the hallway light leading to the stairs. Now in semidarkness, the effect made the fireplace and candlelight eerie, dancing against the walls and producing shadows made by us. It was just about five on a bleak Saturday afternoon, but the shortening days made the outside beach appear as twilight.

Dave, who sat next to me, facing Joy across the table, nudged me.

In the semidarkness, I glanced at him.

His eyes pointed at the chair behind Joy.

My eyes followed his.

THE CHAIR.

Despite the fact that the chair was right next to the fireplace, with a roaring fire of four logs, it was in darkness. It was placed right near the stone hearth and should have been lit by the fire-light and the three-wick candle on the hearth.

I looked at Joy as she began to address the chair, ignoring Dave. It appeared she was murmuring a prayer, her face in shadow. Joy then began to raise her voice: "Whoever is here with us, please give us a sign."

Our fingers rested on the bottom of the small glass, waiting.

Silence.

Joy intoned again, "Whoever is with us, give us your name."

Silence.

Bernice withdrew her finger, shaking her arm.

Joy opened her eyes. "You have to keep your finger on the glass," she told Bernice.

Then the glass moved.

Skimming over the surface of the board before Bernice could place her finger back, it went to the letter *G*.

"G," said Joy. Bernice's finger joined ours.

The glass moved to *O*. "O," said Joy.

Silence.

"Go where?" Joy asked.

Silence.

Then the glass cup moved again.

"G"

"O"

"Please tell us where to go."

Silence.

Then a breeze sent a chill behind me.

I turned, glancing at the stairwell, where there was a light. Denise looked, following my line of sight. Dave shifted to look behind us.

"That's probably the draft from the stairs," said Lucas.

"Please keep from talking," Joy said.

"Spirit, tell us where to go." Joy again.

Denise took her finger off. "My arm's freezing in this position." She began shaking it.

The rest of us followed as Denise asked for a break.

It had been at least thirty minutes.

Bernice: "What did GO mean?"

We sat shaking our arms, freeing up the spasm of the position we had been in, with one arm extended.

The glass cup MOVED.

Joy's eyes, now open, became large. "Who's moving it?!"

I gawked as the cold entered the room.

Denise, then Lucas, then Trey stood.

The glass stopped.

"Okay, Joy. Can you..." Dave.

Joy replied, "Let's all put our fingers on it again, people!"

We all placed one finger on the glass bottom.

Then it happened.

The glass began to move in earnest, skimming the surface.

"G"

"O"

"Go?" (Joy)

It moved to the word "Yes."

"Yes." (Joy)

It moved again to yes.

"Where?" (Dave)

Then the glass moved rapidly, our fingers almost straying with the quick unexpected movement.

"A"

"W"

"A"

"Y"

Joy's face mirrored shock.

"Away!" Joy said in a loud voice.

"Go away," Dave clarified.

The glass flew across the table and into the fireplace, shattering the glass.

The candle blew out.

The light from the stairwell winked off.

Darkness.

The fireplace logs began to weaken, plummeting the room in an even deeper dark.

I stood, ready to run.

"Dave." This was Denise. She was looking at the chair.

"You see it? Elise?"

Joy turned to look behind her at the chair. "Someone's here."

I looked away, stood. I moved out of the circle and reached for the crucifix on my chest, pulling it out.

Joy shot up and moved away from the table. Her eyes were wide.

The plastic wrapping ripped off the windows.

The windows slammed open, blasting cold air.

A wind blew the board off the table.

I was out the door – down the steps with Dave and Bernice at my heels.

The tide was gaining.

Gusts.

As we turned to look back at the house from the sand, Denise was running down the front steps, grasping her coat.

Trey, Lucas and Dave's roommates followed us at the rear.

The screen door slammed back and forth.

Dave ran back for Joy, who finally exited down and onto the sand, joining us.

Dave looked pointedly at me. "Did you see her?"

"I... I don't want to see."

I realized I had been shaking even before the chill had set in the room, despite the roaring fireplace.

Without a coat on, I caught myself still holding onto the crucifix around my neck.

Joy was terrified. "I have to go back and use the bathroom. You guys get your coats, and I'll get the rest of the stuff."

"What about the chair? You can't leave that damn thing in

there!" Trey was terrified, in awe, looking at the house as if it were on fire.

Lucas ran in. Joy followed.

Minutes later, they both reemerged. Joy had the board, folded it, and wrapped it in a blanket: "I can't destroy it. It will have to be stored somewhere safe."

Lucas was carrying the chair. Dave met him, and they both carried it towards the waterline.

"Let the tide carry it away." Lucas backed away.

They all turned to me.

"What do we do with it?" Denise asked, her eyes bulbous and glistening with fear – or the cold.

"Let the water take it."

"You can't destroy it. It would make HER angry." Joy was adamant.

We huddled, watching the tide near the chair, as if some force would decide for us.

The waves were gaining.

"Let it go where it wants." I turned away, dismayed.

Everyone followed as I turned my back, facing the porch door, away from the winds. We had to go back inside eventually. Then, through the open windows, I saw the light from the stair-well come back on.

The house was a mess. Trey and Lucas, with our help, dried the floors, shut and secured the windows, and placed the plastic back on.

Our evidence: the shattered shot glass, still in the fireplace. Through the glass door, we watched the chair sitting at the edge of the surf, the water lapping at its legs.

"Someone call the landlord." It was Denise, pragmatic as ever.

I moved out of the dorm at the end of the semester shortly before Christmas break. I joined Denise in the upperclassmen dorm across campus and well away from Saint Justina Hall in the spring. The room held a bad vibe after that. A year later, Dave and I returned with Joy to the flea market, hoping to locate the vendor who sold me the chair. We never found him, so the origins of the chair remain a mystery.

Trey moved to a neighboring town, where he joined two other art majors in an old Victorian house. The experience of the seance made Trey, the more adventurous of the two, curious. Lucas, born from a superstitious family, would not return to the beach house and only stayed a week after our seance. He contacted the landlord, who had a trash company haul it away, as even the tides would not take it. Lucas moved to an upper-classman dorm.

The Victorian house Trey subsequently rented with two other students was reported to be haunted by a girl who used to cast spells in the attic of the house. The girl's mother reportedly saw a creature with talons, which followed her to her car. When Trey returned to the beach house with Lucas one last time and scanned the house for any debris or remaining furniture, he invited him to the new "digs" – the Victorian house – and Lucas declined after hearing of its history.

Trey kept in touch through the years, moving to Mass-achusetts to attend med school and eventually to Canada, where he's a practicing psychiatrist. His story of the haunted Victorian house he rented with two other men, both artists, is in a future nonfiction novel, *The Talisman*.

The last and final story in this compilation comes from Trey's father, "George," who ran an antique store in neighboring Rhode Island. It's uncanny how small the world can be, as the issues at his father's shop began around the time I finally disposed of the haunted chair.

PART II

THE CHINOISERIE URN

CHAPTER 11

I t was all about timing. When Augustina entered the shop in Cordoba, she recognized her great-grandfather's trademark ceramics. If she had entered a week later, she would not have seen them, as tourists usually came in droves, in buses, taking every piece of earthenware as if they were priceless. They sold that quickly. After three generations of ceramic makers, she was the first to move away into the Barcelona area and take a job unrelated to her ancestral roots: accounting.

Then she met an American and found herself moving to the US, to New England, in a small coastal town and running a store: an antique shop that had been in her husband's family for a few generations. That was all about timing too. If she had not been working in Barcelona at that particular store, standing by the front door instead of inside in the accounting office where she usually could be found, she would not have met him, the American antique dealer from New England.

Augustina's degree in business came in handy, as she did the books, the legal stuff that makes a store a store, and was content. However, she had to learn all about antiques, a realm totally new to her. Especially fine china: how rare, when it was manufactured, how many of each style, and when the marks on the bottom, or handle or whatever, changed. What made it a quality object, precious and coveted highly in comparison to others. Her husband, Stanley, a curator and avid golfer, piled book upon book on Augustina related to the craft. Books on art history, antique art, furniture, porcelain, etcetera.

She loved the jewelry in particular, as she adored wearing the ornate pieces, and then there was the fine bone china. While he played golf in the summer sun where the Kennedys in their sporty V-necks used to play, she touched and marveled at every piece of jewelry that came lovingly wrapped or set in satin.

Years later with two teens in the house, Augustina was a proud antique dealer in her own right, and travel around the world she did, with Stanley, a comfortable American couple of means. They cultivated an eye for the unusual, valuable and rare.

However, once in a while Augustina indulged by seeking pieces that were "fun": vintage objects that were not yet antiques, but complemented the decor. She had begun a chinoiserie collection: blue and white porcelain pieces of Chinese origin. It was a game of sorts to determine which ones were fakes, vintage, or older with value. Her parties were hits when the guests marveled at which pieces were "authentic" and which were from contemporary decor shops.

Towards the end of one particular winter, Augustina was in a small street in far-off Krakow, Poland, when an object caught her eye: a large urn. The piece, she learned from the shop, had been made prior to World War I. Augustina returned to their hotel and researched the urn, wary of the vendor she had not met before. It was from the Qing Dynasty. The shopkeeper, a man of Hungarian descent, indicated it was from the late 1800s, procured from a house sale at the end of World War II.

She did a double take when she returned to inspect it in

more detail, now with Stanley in tow. It looked to be in perfect condition, almost as if it were new. Stanley was not too eager to purchase it, as it was expensive and appeared to be only a few years old. However, Augustina was so eager to have it that he eventually gave in despite his misgivings. Perhaps, he agreed, it was just that – expensive because it was in perfect condition. So perfect, he indicated, though a studied look in his eyes gave away an apprehension. But give in he finally did after he negotiated a better price and the vendor agreed.

That done, they made arrangements to ship it and took the certificate of authenticity back to the room for further research. However, as with any avid buyer, eagerness made them neglect to open the urn and inspect the interior, as any dealer would.

The vendor, a man used to heavy drink, buxom like a woman, with soft hands and a predilection for heavy sweaters, marked the urn's shipping label first class. He encased it in bubble wrap and carefully blanketed it in layer upon layer of crumpled Polish newsprint. It was insured, vetted and handled with great care.

CHAPTER 12

A large brown box, three times the size of the family dog's crate, emerged from the back of the UPS truck. When the parcel man rang, he peered at a hallway with high ceilings, heavy mahogany paneling, and sconces on the walls. A large and stately brownstone house wrapped by a garden with a black wrought-iron fence greeted the UPS man, who stood waiting with a clipboard.

At the front door, a very meticulous petite Filipina woman, Vilma, smiled and opened the door. She had been with the couple for decades and had supervised one babysitter after another when the couple's younger daughter was still a small child. With both children now beginning college, Vilma was now left to herself while Augustina and Stanley traveled to procure antiques or keep hours at the shop. This was one of those quiet afternoons, after grocery shopping, when Vilma had the house to herself to do some mending she had been putting off and even walk the dog, Mops, a large Bernese mountain dog.

Vilma had just started mending her own clothing, spendthrift as she was, when the doorbell gave off its distinct chime.

The dog followed her as she descended the stairs, her slippered feet padding on the carpeted steps.

When she opened the door, the UPS man was at the ready, his clipboard and pen paused in midair for her to sign. He had a look of frustration on his youthful face as if she had taken too long to respond. She signed after glancing at the correct address, and he proceeded to recount how the box was incredibly heavy as if it were resisting his attempt to take it out of his truck. Vilma then asked if he would help her bring it in, as she herself, now in her late forties, had a bad back. The man looked at his watch, leaned down and nudged the package with a hand as if to awaken it from slumber. He said it might in fact be too heavy for both of them to carry over the threshold. "No, we'll just drag it across the floor, if necessary," she said. "It's too valuable to sit on the front step."

Vilma put her hands on both sides of the box as he reached under to support the weight from falling, giving her the lighter end of the deal. The box proved lighter than she thought. She looked back at the youth in amazement, wondering what, if anything, could be wrong with him.

As soon as the box was in the foyer, the Bernese began barking in alarm from behind her. He had been watching from the sidelines since the bell rang and was now in a frenzy, whining and barking as if an intruder had entered the home. Vilma, who rarely heard the dog bark, a quiet and affable breed by nature, stood watching, perplexed. She wondered, she later recounted, if the dog needed to get out to do his business.

She quickly wove her way through the large house, heading for the back door by the kitchen, calling out to Mops to come and exit. Mops would not cease furiously jumping at Vilma's Japanese-style apron as he followed. Staining it, almost, the creases undulating as his large paws made contact with the starched fabric. Vilma heard the truck pull away from the gate, leaving the box inside the open front door.

"I am afraid," Vilma told Augustina later in her precise use of the English language when she returned from shopping. "Mops never barked like that."

Augustina was used to Vilma's nature, a woman raised in the far-off provinces of southern Philippines who was shy and fearful by nature. "Nonsense," she replied. "It's just a strange scent for Mops. It's new to the house, and he will get used to it." Augustina entered the kitchen and saw the dog inside his crate, like a large panda that had been scolded, frowning a dog's frown and whining.

Then, leaving Vilma to prepare dinner, Augustina strode to the drawing room and stopped at the door, where she saw the large unopened box sitting on the carpet near the grand piano. Vilma, true to her strength, had been able to move the box away from the front foyer.

CHAPTER 13

The French doors were open, the dimming light from the patio casting a glow over the huge box. Augustina was excited that it came, right on time to display it for her little luncheon party later that week. She strode over to her chinoiserie by the bay windows of the sitting room to examine where she could place the urn, and then went back to the drawing room. That was when she hesitated, wondering what was amiss.

Then there was the stillness. Too still. "The hairs on my arms," she said, "despite the last warm rays of the sun on the patio nearby, were standing like static." She walked past the box, out onto the flagstone patio, surveying the garden of fruit trees: apples, pears and an arbor of grapes. At first, she thought perhaps there was a lightning storm coming that afternoon, which could account for the silence and the static. *What's the matter with me?* she thought. "The silence was etched in my ears like thick cotton." She clarified that it was like when she was a child who suffered through an ear infection.

Then she realized she, like Vilma, had an inexplicable fear

suddenly throb in her heart. She surveyed the garden, feeling, watching – her sides up like the hackles of a dog.

Here and there the bird feeders were full of wheels of seeds. Nary a bird on them.

Afraid of what?

"I inhaled, then blew out my stress," Augustina said.

She reentered, perplexed and confused. She was basically a calm and composed woman, not easily jarred.

She had become anxious like Vilma the housekeeper of twenty-four years, now a woman in her forties.

Augustina dallied around the box and recounted: "I had just washed my hands, chapped as they were, and reached for the tape on top of the box where the shipping label had been affixed. The return address was from Poland. It was definitely the urn I had so fallen in love with." She peered again at her chinoiserie collection by the bay windows in the next room, sitting at attention like rows of compliant schoolchildren dressed in blues and whites, of different shapes and sizes. Among the plants they sat, merry and hopeful, like dogs waiting to be petted. "Why do I feel so strange when I should be excited like a child on Christmas morning?"

Somehow, the eagerness of the moment, which she usually experienced upon adding another blue and white, wasn't there. She found herself sitting on the piano bench, almost reluctant to open the box. Then the sound of birds chirping amid the rising susurrus of Vilma's and Stanley's voices made the room alive again.

Augustina looked down at the box and began tearing away at the tape.

A sound behind her.

She leaped.

"Dinner's on." It was Stanley.

CHAPTER 14
VILMA

As ma'am and sir ate, I returned to the kitchen and cleaned up; pots and pans I had used, the scouring pad now worn, I replaced. I grabbed the mop from the pantry closet and almost screamed when the mouse came running from between the rice bag and potatoes. Oh no. I put the bag higher up on the shelf and made a note to buy some traps, deliberating to myself when to tell the missis about the mice. She would not like it, nor would sir, who is very clean and very particular about cleanliness. Mops would not like it either.

Speaking of Mops, I mopped the stone floor, wished I had brought back a "bunot" or coconut husk with me on my last visit to the Visayas, my hometown near the water outside Cebu. The husk made the floor shine and outdid what a stupid mop would do. Oh well. I mopped and mopped, adding Mr. Clean, then rinsed, and by then the dog was getting frisky and impatient. I let Mops out the back door, then ma'am was ready and summoned me to clear the dining table.

It was now my turn to eat. So I took my plastic plate, my large spoon, dug into the casserole I made, and sat on the stool facing the large back garden. Mops was doing what dogs do:

sniff and pee. But then he suddenly ran to the side of the house where I could no longer see him.

Mops was barking furiously again. It sounded like he was near the French doors in the drawing room by the piano. Actually, it sounded like he was tearing into something by the French doors.

I stood from my stool, hoping he was busy digging somewhere in the garden, which was not like him either, but I knew tearing when I heard it.

I walked out the kitchen door, made my way around the house, past the cherry tree that had a huge nest of wasps to be removed, past the dead peach tree that was sitting in the middle of the three-seater corner benches – and then saw Mops.

He had stopped barking.

Mops was sitting and watching.

He was very still and looked bigger than he was.

Then I realized it was because all his fur was standing.

Something just inside the French doors INSIDE the drawing room was tearing at the box.

I approached in my slippers, the back flop of my flip-flops flicking against my heels. Too cold for flip-flops, but it was my slippers, and I liked what I was accustomed to.

There was an animal tearing at the box. Its back was a very dark color.

It turned at the sound of my breath.

What is that?

A huge pair of eyes, pupils wide.

Madre de Dios.

I ran.

I heard my voice screaming.

Back to the kitchen – then turned – back to the garden.

I must get Mops.

I cannot leave Mops.

It was bigger than Mops.

I grabbed Mops as I looked at the creature. I dragged Mops by the collar.

It turned its back to me and kept tearing away.

So heavy is Mops.

Mops finally followed me – into the kitchen, through the door...

I shut it, turned the lock and turned.

Missis was there. Mister was there.

Both standing in the kitchen, looking pale.

Mops had a smell on him. Clinging on his fur.

"He smells like crap," said missis. "What was out there?"

"It's inside the house!"

Then mister ran.

Missis ran behind him.

CHAPTER 15

The drawing room was a mess. Polish newsprint was strewn all over the drawing room carpet, the Persian design obscured by small scraps of the foreign newsprint torn into a million pieces. The plastic bubble wrap, or what remained of it, was flying in the breeze, some glinting in the fading light of the open French doors; some clung with static to the furniture.

Stanley secured the doors, surveyed the area, and darted up the steps to locate the creature. Shortly, he returned and helped Vilma pick up the papers, the plastic bubble wrap, and pieces of the cardboard box. "Whatever you saw is no longer here."

Vilma looked up. "Where do you think it went, sir?"

Augustina approached the box. There on one corner where she had pulled the tape off, a hole had been made. Whatever did it had claws, the long scratch marks still evident on the box's sides. Cored.

Augustina peered into the hole the animal had made.

Inside was the urn, the intricate blue and white design staring back at her.

She sat on the carpet, pulling at the remains of the box,

widening the hole. Finally, all sides were down, and the urn was in view.

She looked at her hands, which were filthy with some type of soot. She inspected the urn.

Stanley raised a hand, covering his nose. "No scratches?"

"I smell it," said Vilma, a look of disgust on her face.

Augustina stood, dusting off the soot from her pants. "I need to wash my hands and change."

Vilma gingerly approached the urn and touched the lid, inspecting it.

"Is the top closed?"

She struggled to turn the lid and open it. "It will not open. Where do you want it, missis?"

Augustina walked away. "Just put it near the chinoiserie in the next room, please. I'm taking a shower."

Stanley stood, watching Vilma struggle with the urn. He appeared puzzled. "Vilma, go ahead and wash the dog, please. I will take care of this." Stanley picked up the urn and carried it out of the room as Vilma followed Augustina, who was dismayed.

Vilma approached Mops, took him by the collar, and pulled him through the French doors and out to the garden. "You smell, boy. That was a big skunk."

Vilma turned on the hose, rinsing the dog. Behind her, watching in shadow by the corner of the stone wall, was a dark form.

Vilma hummed a tune and wondered why Mops was whining as she shampooed his thick fur. If a dog could look frightened, he did, she surmised as she rinsed his fur from head to toe.

Just inside in the sitting room, Stanley was admiring the urn now positioned next to the chinoiserie. His eyes traveled to Vilma through the French doors that lined one side of the house, overlooking the patio and the garden beyond. He caught sight of something dark and moving, watching Vilma.

Its eyes, yellow with pupils, made contact with him.

Stanley stood back in surprise, accidentally hitting the urn with his foot.

When he looked up again, whatever it was had disappeared.

Stanley turned the lock on the French door open, exiting quietly. "Vilma, come in and dry Mops in the kitchen. Quickly."

CHAPTER 16

It was all about timing. Augustina watched her husband recount what he had seen while he stood watching Vilma wash Mops in the patio by the garden. She watched from her dresser, the beveled mirror showing his excited demeanor as she brushed her hair loose from the bun she had tied it up in. "What would that thing have done to Vilma or the dog if you had not been watching? What did it look like?" She wanted to know, as she didn't want anything to attack her lovely dog or her faithful housekeeper. "Did you tell Vilma?"

Stanley looked concerned even as she strode towards him and sat by his side at the edge of the four-poster bed, an antique from Portugal. He didn't want to tell his wife that it was a skunk to allay her anxiety, even though it had certainly smelled up the entire drawing room. Because it certainly wasn't. He began to feel that the dog was being stalked, if that made sense, or that the dog had made some animal angry. Skunks don't stare back at you with such menacing looks in a size that rivaled a Bernese, a dog about 110 pounds full grown. What had attracted the animal to the box? As far as he could tell, there was nothing organic or edible in that box. Or was there? He himself had tried to pry open the top of the urn and now wondered why it was so secure, as if it had been sealed on purpose.

Whatever was inside had attracted a large animal of some type, and Mops was on to it.

Tomorrow, he told her, he would get something to pry loose the top of the urn – then that would tell him, he thought, what animal could be attracted to it. Could it be food? Preposterous. Why would anyone store food in an urn? Why did they not open it at the store?

Augustina shrugged when he asked, at a loss for words. She had no idea. Guilty. Some part of her felt guilty for bringing the urn into the house. They certainly didn't want vermin in the house. "It was probably a racoon looking at you, dear."

Stanley shook his head. "No racoon. It didn't have the markings of one, and that size. They don't grow to that size, Augustina. Not in New England, anyway."

CHAPTER 17

By the rays of the full moon, the patterns on the urn seemed to undulate. It was colored with a blue background with the design of flowers in white – a reversal of color. Hearts rimmed around the top where the lid was secured.

The French doors shook with an unseen wind, the trees outside bending here and there like a swaying dancer. Mops was in his usual bolster bed on the landing of the second-floor hall, fast asleep, stretched out with paws past the bed like a drunken man in a stupor. One side of the hall was a balcony overlooking a view of the French doors in the drawing room below. Farther down the hall, the dressing room, the adjoining bath, and finally, the end of the hall where the master suite of bedrooms were located.

Augustina slumbered fitfully, her face turned in repose towards the window that faced the front entrance where the portico and car garages lay. Stanley was turned away towards the bedroom door. When the door opened, it was, however, Augustina who detected the change in air and the light from the hallway that told her the bedroom door had opened.

Immediately, she sat up and turned towards the door. It was Vilma in shadow. She felt annoyed, not having heard the live-in housekeeper knock, but didn't mention it, as she saw the woman's face was a mirror of fear.

"What's the matter?"

Vilma stood, looking at her, but remained quiet.

"Vilma?"

Then, without a word, Vilma walked out, leaving the door open.

Puzzled, Augustina reached for her robe, put on her slippers, and padded to the door, glancing at the sleeping form of her husband as she passed.

In the hall, she looked towards where the dog lay. Mops sat on his bed, whining. He stood, sauntered over, tail between his legs, and entered the bedroom, leaping onto the bed. Augustina shut the door, leaving the dog with Stanley. Now out in the hall, she looked around and saw that the window at the end of the hall was wide open. Wrapping her robe securely around her, she strode over to the window and called out, "Vilma?"

She looked out the window and down into the side garden. Satisfied, she shut the window and turned the lock. She turned.

On the floor in the middle of the hall sat the urn, near their bedroom door.

She gasped. "Vilma?"

Silence.

Augustina reentered the room, not losing eye contact with the urn, which was only a few feet from the door.

The dog was on her side of the bed, his eyes looking worried.

"Stanley." She nudged him.

"What? What time is it?"

"Vilma was here."

"Why?"

"She brought the urn, and it's right outside."

"Outside? Why..." Stanley sat upright, searching for his glasses. He turned the lamp on. "You're shaking."

Augustina nodded emphatically. "The urn..."

Stanley stood, strode to the door and opened it. Right outside was the urn. "Why did Vilma bring it up here?"

"I don't know. I called her, and she didn't come."

"She probably went back to her room."

Stanley walked out past the urn, and Augustina followed. Mops was right at their heels, as if he didn't want to be alone.

Stanley took the stairs and headed straight past the dining room towards the kitchen, switching lights on as he went. He stopped right in front of an unmarked door next to a pantry with shelves, jars and bottles of foodstuffs.

He knocked. "Vilma?"

Silence.

Augustina approached, knocked. "Vilma, are you there?"

Inside the small room, Vilma awakened and sat up, obviously fast asleep.

"Coming, ma'am." She pulled on her robe.

Outside the door, Stanley and Augustina observed a weary and sleepy Vilma open the door.

"Sorry, Vilma. Were you just upstairs a few minutes ago?" Stanley inquired, eyes adjusting to the dim light of the bedroom.

"No, sir. I went to bed at ten. Why?"

Augustina and Stanley looked at each other.

"You were at the door of our bedroom."

Vilma just stared back at Augustina, puzzled.

Stanley cleared his throat. "Did we wake you?"

"Yes."

Augustina looked at the kitchen clock on the adjacent wall. It was 2:30 a.m. "We woke up and... well... "

The room turned cold.

Vilma glanced back and forth between the couple. A knot formed in her throat. She felt a creepiness she could not shake. "Ma'am, I was in my room here."

Augustina held Mops by the collar protectively and looked towards the second floor.

CHAPTER 18

Celia, green eyed with strawberry blonde hair like Stanley with the face of her mother, had just dragged in her luggage, a large affair, in handsome leather. She looked up to survey the room: late May flowers were in full bloom through the French windows. Celia breathed in as she casually sauntered into her mother's sitting room and sat on the settee, admiring the chinoiserie collection in the dimming glow of the afternoon.

She pulled a large mobile from the pocket of her black jeans, texting. From the corner of her eye, she saw Mops as the dog bounded up at the sight of her, knocking the mobile from her hands. Vilma followed behind.

"Miss Celia, sorry, I didn't hear you. Did you eat? Are you hungry?"

"Starved! Mops almost knocked me over!" She laughed as she petted the beautiful animal, which licked her face.

"I made cabbage soup."

"Awesome. Thanks."

She gave Vilma an affectionate peck on the cheek, and Vilma blushed in response.

Celia grabbed her cell phone from the floor, dusting off some ash that clung from the carpet. The dog sniffed it, pulling back.

Celia ushered the dog towards the French doors to let him out, wiping the ashes on the side of her jeans.

Vilma, in the act of taking the young woman's luggage, placed it down quickly and grabbed the dog's collar. "No, let's keep him inside until we're done, okay?"

Celia paused. "No problem. Everything all right?"

"What's THAT on your jeans?"

"Nothing. Dust, I guess."

Augustina appeared. Celia ran over and, like a small child, hugged and showered her mother with kisses. Mother and daughter examined each other. "Mom, you look good, but you look peaked."

Augustina glanced at Vilma, giving her a knowing look. "Let's eat, and we'll talk."

Celia looked around the room. "Where's Dad?"

"He's taking care of an antique we recently bought."

Vilma had a rag in her hand and started dusting at Celia's jeans.

"Really, Vilma! I took a shower before I got on the train!" Celia laughed.

Vilma glanced at Augustina with a look of apprehension. Augustina examined her daughter's jeans.

"Sorry. It's the dust from the carpet." Celia strode off, leading the group into the kitchen. "I'm starved!"

Vilma followed her down the hall. "We have ham too."

Celia plunked herself down at the large café-style bistro table for six, arranged in the sunroom, where a series of windows looked out onto the back garden. She looked up and marveled at the ceiling, which had a recent addition: Stanley had enhanced the sunroom by placing beveled mirrors on either side of the brass chandelier, one side reflecting a view of the garden beyond, the other, the adjoining kitchen.

"Looks great, Mom."

Augustina joined her daughter at the table, holding a steaming cup of tea, admiring her. She observed Vilma serving the hot cabbage soup with a medley of beef ribs, carrots and ears of corn. Vilma served it in a soup tureen decorated with French dancing lords and ladies: a Limoges piece of china Augustina had acquired from their last trip to the Perigord area of France. The cobalt blue tureen with the dancing lords and ladies complemented the pastel blue and cream theme of the kitchen and adjoining sunroom. Vilma produced a large soup bowl, which she placed in front of Celia in a celadon green color, which exuded elegance, but it was not an antique, Augustina thought. She didn't want to risk using an antique set of dishes for daily use... or just in case it was haunted.

Celia helped herself to the steamy soup, adding fish sauce to the mix to enhance the flavor, a bottle that Vilma used in sauteing all her cooking. Augustina marveled at how her daughter was so knowledgeable about international cuisine and, soon, art history and anthropology, which was Celia's double major. They were companionably eating in silence when Celia insisted on Vilma joining them, as she'd grown close to the loyal housekeeper she'd known as a child. Augustina grabbed a soup bowl and signaled Vilma to join them. Without Stanley there, Augustina felt more relaxed about the social mores he appeared to unwittingly impose when it came to domestic help.

Settled in with the three of them eating in companionable silence, Augustina decided it was as good a time as any to update her daughter on what had been happening during the past few odd weeks, before her younger daughter, Cindy, joined them for the summer break. She didn't want either one caught by surprise in the event that something else happened at the house.

Vilma was in the act of putting away the dishes when Augustina raised her hand to stop her. "Vilma, sit for a few minutes, please. Let's catch Celia up on what's happening."

Celia looked back, attempting to surmise the reason for her mother's cautious tone. "Mom, are you and Dad having problems?"

"Oh, no, no, no!" Vilma replied empathically. Augustina shook her head dismissively at Vilma. She wanted to explain without interruption.

"It's nothing like that, thank goodness. It's about where your father is today because of a purchase we made in haste."

Vilma qualified: "They are arguing more, but it's because of the antique urn."

"Vilma, please." Augustina rolled her eyes.

Celia looked on, now interested. She sat back, arms folded, waiting. Augustina signaled Vilma to remain silent. In response, Vilma stood up to turn on some lights, since the room was now in partial darkness as twilight approached.

Celia watched Vilma as she walked from sconce to sconce, flicking a switch in the dining area, then in the kitchen, where the recessed lights cast a warm glow on the marble countertops and the cobalt blue stove. Celia yawned, stretched, then leaned her head back to stretch her neck, shutting her eyes.

"Go on, Mom. I'm listening. I think we get it. What about..." Celia opened her eyes and made eye contact with the ceiling mirrors.

The dark creature with yellow eyes LOOKED back at her from the mirror's reflection.

Celia bolted upright and looked outside the windows. There it stood, right next to the stone water fountain.

Then it vanished.

"Oh my fucking... MOM!"

Augustina turned and stood right by the window. She turned back to her daughter, who was now white as a sheet.

"What was it?"

"You didn't see THAT?"

Vilma bolted for the kitchen door, turning the lock. Augustina checked the locks on the windows.

"Where's Mops, Mom?!"

They ran out of the room.

CHAPTER 19

Mops busily chewed, paws both firmly placed on a rawhide. He was up in the bedroom hallway, ensconced on his bed. When the women began running, he stood and padded down the stairs.

Celia stopped, relieved, seeing Mops holding his rawhide on the stair landing. She grabbed the rawhide and rubbed his ears. "Glad you're inside."

Augustina dialed her cell phone, now concerned about Stanley's progress on the urn. "Hon, where are you?"

Pause.

"Celia just saw what you saw."

Pause.

"Okay. Be careful when you come back. It's out there."

Minutes later, the women were still excitedly talking when Stanley walked in from the adjoining garage. He sat.

The three women paused, riveted to Stanley.

He cleared his throat. "I talked to Gene, and he's going to look into where the urn came from. We got it open."

"What was inside?" This was Augustina.

"A skeleton."

Silence.

"Of...?"

"A hand."

Vilma darted out of the room.

Stanley continued: "Gene's not a pathologist, but from what he could tell, it looked like a human hand. It was at least perhaps a century old, maybe less."

Augustina paled. "We have to get it back to his or her relatives!"

"It's not that simple, of course. It was stashed in there for some reason, and now we have to have the house cleansed, as it came haunted." Stanley pointed outside, where he had seen the dark creature. "I don't normally believe in stuff like that, but I know what I saw back there."

"I saw something like a huge dog, Dad. Just a few hours ago. Is that what you're referring to?"

"That was probably what Mops reacted to and what tore up the box the urn was in," added Augustina.

Celia looked terrified. "Mom, you said it also appeared in your bedroom."

"It wasn't a dog... something that looked like Vilma. But Vilma –"

Stanley interrupted. "Okay, let's not keep rehashing it. I am hoping Gene hooks up with this woman who knows about the origin of the urn. Once we know, we can move forward with what we have to do next."

"You mean how to get rid of the urn?"

"I got rid of it. It's in Gene's office. The 'thing' here should be gone, but obviously it's still..."

"What do you mean, Dad?"

"That urn came with something. Gene called it a 'guardian spirit.' That's probably what you just saw even though the urn's no longer here."

CHAPTER 20

"This is hocus-pocus!"

Augustina peered into Vilma's bedroom, astounded. The woman had purchased crosses and nailed them to four sides of her bedroom, added pictures of saints all around the walls of her small and spartan room, and a scapular was nailed to the door. Vilma was frantic and asked for them all to vacate the home until whatever plagued them had passed. Augustina told her they would stay, but she was free to go to her sister's if she felt she was safer somewhere else. Loyal as ever, Vilma opted to stay.

She baked cookies and made a cake, busying herself while Stanley discussed what needed to be done, then left unannounced. Later that evening, she returned, praying as she entered, a rosary around her neck, with a plastic bag filled with plastic crucifixes, which she distributed to them. She had just returned from the local parish priest, who had given them to her after they were blessed.

Mops was whining, waiting to be fed, but Vilma, after feeding him, insisted on having him on a leash whenever he went potty, for fear that the creature would return.

While Vilma walked the dog on the street well away from the house, Celia texted as Augustina watched.

"Who are you texting? Cindy?"

"I told her not to come home yet. She's staying with friends until we clear this up."

"Good. Thank you."

"Mom?"

"Yeah?"

"I need you to talk to this lady –"

"What lady?"

"This lady." Celia turned her cell phone around to show a series of text messages.

"Claire, what?"

"She's an angel guide. She can tell us what to do way before Gene."

"You want ME to talk to an angel person?" Augustina gazed back at her daughter in consternation.

"She's a guide. A trained sensitive. Please hold off on the censorship, Mom."

Silence.

"Mom, please. Just give her a try. She might know what to do about a haunted antique. Just in case Gene doesn't come up with a solution."

Behind them, Vilma was removing her jacket, unleashing the dog. "I think I know what it is, ma'am." Vilma was very pale.

"Have you seen it?"

"No, ma'am. But if it imitates me, then it's…"

"What is it, you think?" Celia ventured.

"It's an 'aswang.'"

Celia googled "aswang." She turned the cell phone for her mother to see.

Silence.

"Okay, dear. How do I get a hold of this angel lady?"

CHAPTER 21

A plan had been settled upon before they left for the "angel lady": The house would be left empty to assure no one was left alone. Celia would take Mops and head to see high school friends with her boyfriend, while Augustina and Vilma went to see Claire. Stanley would, as usual, tend to the store.

At night, Celia would sleep in a spare cot in Vilma's room instead of sleeping alone in her room. Celia also moved Mops' dog bed into Vilma's room so the two of them could watch over him. Vilma was glad for the company, and the crosses she'd nailed to all sides of the room gave her some comfort. It allayed Augustina's concern that her housekeeper might entertain leaving their employ for what appeared to be a temporary situation. They would stay together no matter what.

Claire, the "angel lady," was a middle-aged woman who looked like Goldie Hawn, but very serious. Simply dressed in jeans and a woolen sweater that appeared to have been tossed at a thrift store, she commandeered the entire third floor of a Vietnamese restaurant in the Chinatown section of the city.

Augustina negotiated a series of three steep staircases with Vilma in tow.

The door to the suite of rooms on the third floor appeared simple: an apartment that spanned the entire floor, as Claire explained she and her daughter's family, plus in-laws, shared the floor. The in-laws were Vietnamese and owned the restaurant on the ground floor, with the second floor used for storage and bookkeeping. Images of Cao Dai, the religion the family subscribed to, were all over the living areas, particularly a poster of a triangle with an eye in the center.

When Augustina entered with Vilma, the simple and charming woman told them that she'd gotten some background information about the haunted urn from Celia, who was in college with Claire's son, Edwin. Thus the common bond.

The next bond that cemented the arrangement was the fact, according to Claire, that she too had dealt with a family haunting when her grandmother had passed away alone on the second floor of the building, which they now used as a restaurant storage area and break room for the restaurant employees. Her grandmother had dabbled in some form of spiritual practice that had apparently attracted the wrong variety of spirits.

However, the urn was different, as they did not know whose remains were in the urn or the nature of the creature in the garden. The eerie being that had materialized in Augustina's bedroom was a serious concern, as it had been inside the house in the dead of night.

Claire appeared pretty up front and down to earth so much that Augustina immediately felt less suspicious. The woman's demeanor also allayed her fears that the woman might be a charlatan. Even Vilma, who was a staunch Catholic, was immediately impressed by the woman's frankness. She considered the woman a Godsend at a time when they had an evil spirit in the home. Augustina was amazed that Vilma did not become suspicious of the woman, who was essentially a Buddhist. Vilma prodded her employer to share all the stories of their encounters while the woman Claire made tea and lit some sage, which she placed in a pot by the window. It smelled sweet, and Augustina thought it might be marijuana until she saw the stalks, which resembled her own herbal plant in the kitchen.

Claire explained that she normally didn't use sage, but thought it was a Western touch that might put them both at ease. She became more absorbed when Augustina intimated that the doglike creature in the garden had been seen by Stanley as having yellow eyes. Vilma's doppelganger, a dead ringer materializing by the door to the couple's bedroom, was a serious concern, Claire agreeing that it might be an "aswang" or shapeshifter, as Vilma had previously noted.

Then Vilma told her about the skunklike scent the urn came in and the oily "soot" that was all over Augustina's hands, on the carpet, and later clung like glue to Celia's jeans. Claire called it "ectoderm" or "ectoplasm," and Vilma googled it on her mobile. Claire corrected her and indicated it was ectoplasm, usually a substance that was a precursor to the appearance of a spirit.

Claire ushered them into a small dining room, where the windows had a view of the city veiled in a late spring mist. There were Buddhist symbols on the walls and then the triangle with the eye again. Tea was steaming and ready, so as Claire served the tea, she explained that the symbol meant the "third eye" or "discernment," and she felt both Augustina and Vilma had the ability, which allowed them to "see" the creature and then, later, the phantom of Vilma.

Feeling responsible for bringing the situation upon her family, Augustina shared her encounter with the antique urn at a shop in Krakow and regretted how they'd acquired it without thinking of opening the top, which had been sealed for some mysterious reason. In her haste, she hadn't paid attention to her own "third eye," as she'd had a negative feeling upon touching it. Claire listened without interruption and then leaned back, deep in thought.

Minutes passed, and finally the woman spoke. "You're dealing with an evil spirit. It was guarding the urn, and all those signs – the bad smell, the evil creature, the specter of what looked like Vilma, the soot or oily substance – those mean there was something tragic that happened to the person who owned the hand. Evil won over that person and opened a portal to the beyond. It showed itself in the familiar form of your house-keeper here, as it was trying to trick you and break the trust that Vilma had earned."

Vilma clung to Augustina's arm, hanging on like a child in the aftermath of a nightmare. It doubled for Augustina as a form of reassurance that the loyalty was unbroken on Vilma's end.

Claire resumed. "When you brought it to the house, the evil that came with it was angry – being moved and wrapped in a box... so the 'guard' of the urn tore up the box. Then it wanted you to 'see' what you had disrupted."

Augustina appeared compelled to convince Claire they were trying to end the nightmare. "But we're trying to fix that. My husband took it out of the house and into a shop so he can find out how it can be returned."

Claire shook her head. "Everything on earth is a combination of light and dark energies. Where there is more light energy, there is harmony, love and joy."

"I think I know what you may be saying..."

"In this case, there is more dark energy because of what happened to the owner of the hand... so BE the LIGHT."

"How? How can I be the light?"

"Find out what the owner wants. Then bring justice so it may know peace."

"Justice! That's huge!" Vilma commented.

"But the evil presence? Would…" Augustina queried.

"It would leave. It's not attracted to good deeds," Claire assured her.

Augustina: "So by resolving this for good…"

"You bring about good, and good will dissipate the evil." Claire nodded firmly. "But you must not be scared. Evil feeds on fear."

"Okay, we won't. We won't be fearful." Augustina nodded.

"You must fix what you upended regardless of what the evil spirit tries to do."

"Tell us what to do, and we will try."

CHAPTER 22

The urn remained in the basement of the shop until Stanley, with the help of Gene, his assistant, was able to finally connect to the owner of the store in Krakow. The urn itself turned out to be, as they knew, a genuine Qing Dynastic antique. However, as it passed hands, it became a decorative urn owned by a Hungarian family sometime in the 1930s. This family appeared to be of considerable wealth and was a patron of the arts, including providing a venue for exhibits of fine antiques. They lived with opulence and culture in the Buda side of Budapest, a haven of culture and art. Like Augustina and Stanley, the family was respected in the community and entertained a lot. Then World War II descended on Hungary. Despite the news of the invasion of Poland, the family took the massacres with a grain of salt, refusing to believe the enormity of the genocide their neighbor up north was experiencing. Until it was too late.

After Poland fell to German hands, the Reich massacred city after city, village after village, reaching the Hungarian capital, where they looted, raped and laid waste to all the grand palaces and mansions, the restaurants and cultural centers that made the grandeur of Budapest famous. Eventually, the urn came into the possession of fleeing locals who witnessed but survived the brutality of the German forces. Taking the remains of the Hungarian elite whom they envied, the armies not only plundered the homes, but killed and butchered the families in their homes. Filled with hate, the armies of the Reich took goods they coveted and left behind the priceless porcelain, which they considered inferior. In the case of the urn, it had been decorated and made by Chinese artisans. Non-Aryans, in Nazi vernacular. They butchered the owner and his family, reportedly forcing pieces of their remains into the pottery and various vases from far-off China.

Thus, the urn and others like it became vessels for human remains. In this case, the remains of the owner's hand: the atrocity meted upon the generous patron of the arts, whose philanthropic "hands" were a source of envy and hate on the part of the Third Reich.

Once the war ended, the scattered remnants of a life once well-lived were looted, re-owned and resold. The urn, undoubtedly among other objects, was discovered and salvaged as a piece of antique by locals. Somehow, it made its way south to Poland and eventually to an antique shop in Krakow. Sealed and unopened until the next owner.

Although the dealers Augustina, Stanley and their colleague Gene were able to discover the urn's history, they were unable to locate the owner of the skeletal remains. The Hungarian store owner had come upon it at an outdoor venue. Unable to track down the family or find out if anyone was still alive, they decided to give the skeletal hand, resealed in the urn, a Catholic burial. Stanley flew to Budapest with the urn as a hand-carry, praying he would be protected as he flew. There, he met with the shop owner who had sold the urn to them, and together they made arrangements to inter it in a cemetery for victims of the holocaust.

As soon as the rites were given and Stanley gave his last respects, the visions of the specter in the garden, the scents and the ectoplasm disappeared back in Massachusetts. Vilma's image no longer showed itself anywhere in the house. Vilma remained at the house, now content to wash the dog in the garden and take him for walks without looking over her shoulder. Celia is now an anthropology professor in her own right, specializing in folklore and world religions. It was opportune for Celia to return home for summer break when all the phantoms were manifesting from the urn. She provided the solution. It was all about timing.

PART III

THE LITHOGRAPH

*Lithography – "A printing process using a flat stone or
metal plate in which the image areas are worked
using a greasy substance so that the ink will
adhere to them while the nonimage areas are
made water-repellent." – The Tate Gallery*

CHAPTER 23

SAM

"When I first saw that print, boy," he said, "that's going to sell on the first day." Dan chuckled, looking professorial as usual in his rimless glasses and trimmed beard. He sat content at our dinner table, awaiting dessert. I chuckled back in the company of old friends, comfortable with the rituals that come with aging in the company of each other.

Outside, the streetlights reflected the settling frost that had just begun to accumulate on the narrow street. Stone and brick homes sat waiting for more of winter's grace. I stood up to grab more wine, and surveyed the two-tier pedestal of cakes and sweets as I passed the pale celadon green sideboard from the Vaucluse region of France. The array of cakes glinted, made more gracious by the vintage Royal Albert china, a rare one, called "Midnight Rose." Two tiers of deliciousness. I reached for the twenty-five-year-old Bordeaux and pulled the corkscrew from the baker's rack.

The chandelier accentuated my wife Alice's gold-flecked diamond studs as she cleared away the dinner dishes, with the ever-helpful Melinda, Mel for short, Dan's wife of twenty-two years. With two kids both in college, they had reached the pinnacle of a career, like us, as dealers of antiquities. My beautiful children were also all grown, with their large hands and feet and the rest of their bodies off to some college, my wallet in their pockets and my heart full of memories.

Time ticked fast for us, running away with our youth, with our own parents feeling even older, like the vintage items and antiques we sell. Businessmen and businesswomen they were, my parents, the grandparents of our children. We travel, buy, sell and collect all the world's heirlooms, misplaced objects of great rarity and value.

As we talked business, Dan fell into a nostalgic moment as he lifted a forkful of mille-feuille, a French pastry made with layers of filo dough. I poured more wine as Alice signaled with one hand to stop. I smelled the coffee brewing and corked the bottle, almost gone.

Dan had been studying me. Finally, he leaned over conspiratorially and whispered, "Would you like the rare print?"

"But I thought it would sell in a flash?" I asked, surprised.

Dan exchanged a nervous tic, a strange one in the world of tics when a couple, used to their ways, mimic each other's facial expressions. Mel replied with a tic across the table as she sat back down to reach for a cake.

"It would. But I think it's best if you had it, as it's your style."

"Where did you find it, again?"

"Some shop on our last trip to New York. It's a lithograph from some Middle Eastern country." That tic again.

Mel ticked back, a tad nervous.

"Did you bring it?" I said.

"It's in the store. I'm giving it to you, we decided."

I was taken aback. We didn't usually give away antiques unless it was a special occasion. This was just dinner at the end of a hectic month. "Dan, how much?"

"Seriously, I'm giving it to you."

Alice sat back down, arms on the table, pensive. "How old is it?"

"It's old. Believe me."

Mel nodded in agreement. "It's at the store, but Dan can drop it off next week."

Alice smiled. "Oh, Mel. That's too generous of you both."

Dan winced. "It needs to be wrapped – protected from the elements."

"Of course," I said.

"It must be pretty special. Are you sure?" Alice ventured.

"Yes, we are." That tic again.

"You can hang it at your shop or keep it covered." Dan glanced at Mel when he said this.

"I'll hang it here at home. It's a gift from friends."

A few weeks later, a parcel arrived and was left at our front door. I opened it immediately, and there it was. A framed lithograph of a castle, a grand one like you would see somewhere in France or Germany, with spires and turrets... and a girl on a swing, in the act of swinging, in the foreground. Pale, muted tones as if it was painted in watercolors. Beautiful.

I called Dan to thank him and got his message machine. "Dan, it's exquisite. I must give you something for this."

Days went by and no callback from Dan.

Well, thank you, Dan, I thought. So generous of you. This looked very expensive, if not rare. 1800s, it seemed, or even older. Strange that the artist didn't sign it.

I showed it to my parents, who smiled but didn't really look, as they were both getting cataract surgery.

"That's great, son. It's great to have good friends in the business."

I hung the framed lithograph, proudly showcased in the drawing room by the baby grand where my father usually sat when they visited us here in Kittery. That was where Dad sat after we picked them up from the hospital – after both Mom's eyes were as clear as a pristine stream after her surgery. She marveled at how she saw now with the eyes of a child – and how like a child saw everything again, greedily taking in everything like a candy store on a Saturday outing. She entered the drawing room, enthralled with what she could see, and paused when she got to the print. Dad walked over, one eye clear, the other still awaiting surgery. He too peered at the lithograph. Then he frowned as she froze.

That was the last time I talked to Mom.

And then they were dead.

CHAPTER 24

I tried as best I could to get rid of it. That was why I was there again in the late fall of 2011, when everything and everyone was gone, dead or dying, like THIS, our old parents' summer house at the edge of Bar Harbor. The house itself seemed to be dying, not literally, but unless I got it repaired, it might in fact fall apart like my parents did.

In the space of one summer, one suddenly had a heart murmur, and then the next week, that pale and dry summer, the pale and dry rose garden of my mother finally yielded buds – and my mother gave way to a heart attack right after her cataract surgery. RIGHT AFTER she studied THAT lithograph. Dad died right after her, and my siblings thought it was from a broken heart. Now they were both gone, and my heart too was broken, feeling betrayed by their sudden deaths and the betrayal of two good friends who gave us a gift we did not want. Why?

First, I needed to sell what was my children's grandparents' summer abode, being the oldest. It was cold enough, and no one – Jerry, Siobhan or me – wanted to drive up there, to this town, this house, which presented us with an even briefer summer than Kittery. None of the kids liked it back then and even now.

Jerry's girls hated the drafty isolation. Siobhan was Siobhan. My two natural siblings, who came shortly one year after another after I was adopted, agreed we should sell it. Sam, Jerry and baby sister Siobhan always agreed on everything.

Since the parental summer house was always dark, dreary and cold, I thought I'd bury the print up there. Like attracts like. A dark, dreary place deserved a dark, dreary print.

> *Forgive me, Mom. Dad, I know you wouldn't and would call it a waste to do that to a rare antique. Our values are just so vastly different. You'd say sell the print – that lithograph – but Alice and I just want it gone. It is just way too coincidental how you saw that print right before you both died. But there's more, Mom and Dad. The lithograph WALKED back to the house. "Really, Sam, our beloved son?" Yes, I can almost hear you ask that question, Mom. I never did get to ask you what you saw, Mom.*

Now, it was too late.

CHAPTER 25

Alice left work early, ridden with a headache she couldn't shake. She ascended the stairs to our bedroom, shaking off her work outfit with the tartan pants and houndstooth scarf I had given her last Christmas.

She slipped into a comfortable jogging suit with a pink hoodie borrowed from Jean, our older daughter now in Salve Regina, majoring in Art History. Then she decided to take a nap and opted for the comfortable sofa facing the fireplace in the family room. Across from her she had a view of the baby grand and the rest of the drawing room beyond.

Around two p.m., I got a call on my cell. "Hon, are you busy?"

"Alice, feeling better?"

An intake of breath. "I am, but I need to ask you a question."

"Go ahead."

"I thought you hung that lithograph in the store?"

I paused, walked out from behind the counter, and looked across the adjacent room, where several articles of furniture sat. I eyed it on the wall, warily approaching as I held the cell to my ear.

I stood a few feet away, managing not to stare too long. "I did. I'm looking at it."

Silence.

"I'm looking at it NOW."

A creepiness inched up my spine as I heard Alice's voice tremble.

I breathed in. "Take a picture and text it. Now."

"Okay."

Silence.

A chime issued from my mobile. I looked down.

"There."

It was THE lithograph.

The drawing room wallpaper of fleur de lis showed behind the corners of the framed print.

Perturbed, discomfited, in awe. Words that describe me in that moment of silent hysteria. No.

"Alice, don't look at it. I'm coming home."

I put the cell phone down, examining the unexaminable. I compared it against what Alice just texted to me as an image. How could we have two now? What the hell?

I glanced around, making sure there were no customers, not even my manager, at the store. Then I took it off the wall. Face down and into a drawer behind the counter. I locked it. Then I drove home, my head swimming.

At home I had torn it from its nail and told Alice a lie: Yes, hon, I forgot to bring it to the store. Sorry, hon, I was so busy I am now getting forgetful. Behind her, I tried to tear it up. Then – I looked at it. It wasn't the same print. Fuck this. It evaded my hands, flying to the floor. I smashed the empty frame, glass shattering onto the wool carpet. Sorry, Alice. Butterfingers today. Tired. She walked away.

Then I looked at the print again. It was a child's crayon drawing. Jean's. I was destroying my own daughter's third-grade art.

Fuck, I was now hallucinating. Alice was now hallucinating. My parents must have been hallucinating.

I think not.

I promised myself it would go even though it was rare.

There was only one place left. Your summer house, Mom. Sorry.

I buried the dratted print by your rosebushes, Mom, after what Alice and I experienced. A twin lithograph. Yeah, right. We were only given one even if there may have been a dozen. Impossible. How could it be? A static image duplicating itself and bilocating?

Nope. Alice will NEVER know this.

NEVER.

It would scare the living crap out of her.

What the hell did you give us, Dan? What the fuck did I ever do to you? DON'T LOOK AT IT, Alice. Please. Should I tell you it's changing right before my eyes?

So I buried it up there – THAT summer house where you dreamed of your golden years, Mom and Dad. We're selling your property anyway. We're not being ungrateful.

Believe me, I tried to sell it. BUT we were just about breaking even – ever since a bunch of customers saw...

Fuck you, Dan.

Mel, you knew it too.

Fuck you.

CHAPTER 26

I placed it in the inglenook, turned some lights on in the cold, drafty kitchen, alone with my thoughts. I had not slept since I buried it up here just to get rid of it since it wouldn't tear. I almost forgot about it, and then one night I thought – could've sworn it was lying on the floor of our bedroom. What kind of paper wouldn't tear? What kind of print would walk back to our house from being buried an hour or more away? What kind of print would return to us when I had hung it at the store?

I had to come out just to make sure it was deteriorating. Paper does that. I even took it out of the frame and all. I swear the print came back, like a cat that was tossed miles away and found its way home.

I picked it up. *Don't look.* I rolled it up. Stuck the print between two large logs, threw some leftover coal from the last family barbecue in Ogunquit into the mix, and lit it. Up the fire went, with all three logs ablaze, reflecting the golden brass of the fireplace screen. Crack, crack, crack.

I sat back on the verdigris-stained Turkish carpet and gawked at my L.L. Bean duck shoes, which in my haste I'd

neglected to take off in the mudroom. Duck shoes were important. I didn't care. I was tangential, and it helped me relax. Got
my mind off the dratted print. Then the grass on the shoes: grass
sticks to everything, and the offensive, though practical shoes
just made green striation marks on the wool. Mom would've
been furious, knowing how she felt about the carpet. I'd have to
roll it up and sell that too, though it wasn't an antique like the
rest of the furniture in the house we all grew up in.

The grass stains were also all over my sweater, which was
undoubtedly from my efforts to dig out what I had buried weeks
ago. I just had to dig it up and make sure it had degraded. But
degraded, it didn't. What kind of paper was it on? I wondered.
The print was still as vivid as when I took it out of the frame. So
I was wet, dirty and feeling like a grave digger on a Friday afternoon. Or someone who went clamming. Hmm… clams. Gotta
get some of that. Focus.

I went to look out the window, then turned on the lamps and
looked out again. In the gloaming, I could still see the Volvo,
which was blue, turn almost black in the menacing dark. My
head hurt, pounding to the tune of some melody I was drowning
to grasp and recall fully. Stress does that.

I went back to the fireplace, and that was when I saw what I
could only describe as sinister: The print somehow flew out of
the fireplace and was now lying on the carpet right where I had
just sat a few minutes ago. Totally unblemished by the fire.
Stretched out like I never rolled it. I approached it and prepared
to pick it up by the edges, but I couldn't get myself to look at it, as
it was faceup. What would I see this time?

Just then, someone was pounding on the door.

I took a few long strides, now high with what must be a lack
of sleep. Or too much driving. I thought it was my parents'
neighbor from the farm.

A man, beard unkempt, tobacco breath, sounding hoarse.

Yup. The farmer next door.

"Hey."

"Hi. Am I disturbing you?" I asked.

"Heck no. I'm Bill. I live up the..."

"Uh, hi. Yeah. Bob."

"No, Bill. Just checking, as I saw a light and thought they were gone."

"Yeah. I'm here cleaning up."

His smile turned into a semblance of sadness. Like he thought they were still alive and was surprised. "I'm... sorry for your loss."

"Thank you. It was quick."

"Uh, for both of them?"

"Ummm... heart attacks."

He nodded, looking around the framed door. His corduroy shirt was partly open, exposing what must have been an under-shirt that hadn't seen a clothes washer in months. "Okay. Call me if you..."

"Thank you. Just getting something to eat..."

He waved like he was on a ship setting to sail. "Okay."

"Have a good night."

Now what was I doing? Oh, yeah.

The castle in the background, turrets and flags, as before, as it always was, even on the day my "friend" acquired it for the shop. Now he won't even drive over let alone stay for dinner despite Alice's great cooking and friendship with Mel. What sticks, sticks. It was stuck with me, and I didn't want any part of it. It really, truly scared the crap out of Mel. Oh, thanks, Dan. Some friend you proved to be. I told you his name, Mom and Dad, but don't dare mention it, as everyone knows him in the antique world. My world. Well, crap, after this, who knew what world I'd be in.

It was the foreground of the picture that bothered me. The

one closest to the viewer. Closer. To. Me. I didn't recall seeing a couple there, standing like ramrod-straight beings from a bad alien movie. They were both looking right at the viewer: Me. No. This was not right. There was something wrong with their eyes. No pupils. As if it were some old horror film I was forced to see with friends as a teenager. What was there before? They looked dressed and looked like Mom and Dad. No. I knew I was tired. Couldn't be. I should have held onto the picture of "the picture" Dan gave me when he bought it at an auction somewhere in New York, he said. He won't even look at it now. He saw something that really and truly got him running out the door and into his car. What truly frightened me was that he wouldn't tell me what he saw or what Mel saw. He told me its value though. Finally, that got me running to sell it. So now what he was running from, I now had with me.

CHAPTER 27

I was exhausted. I was seeing things. I would bury it again. Not tonight, but come morning. No way in hell's bells was I going out there. Especially alone. Alone or with someone like Dad's neighbor Brock or Bill or Bob with the ever filthy undershirt – he would just spread the news that the damn thing was that. Damned. So, Sam, what were you doing in your parents' backyard digging at ten at night? Couldn't it wait until morning? Why in such a hurry? Maybe some pancakes first with grade B maple syrup from Jeannie's with the blue and white striped awning? Just checking. The lights were on, Sam.

So morning it is, I would rebury it and sprinkle it with some holy water Alice gave me. Don't worry, Brock or Bill or Bob, I'm not gossip fodder, and keep those pigs of yours outta my yard. My parents' yard, rather. You with the filthy shirt.

Focus. Maybe that was what it was. I forgot to put holy water on top of it before I buried it. Let me try that.

Alice was good that way. So resourceful, my Alice, thinking of the holy water. She would know, as she's the good Roman Catholic who raised our children. Me, what did I know? I was a Muslim, though not practicing as much as when my birth parents were alive. That would have made me five. Barely five, when they fled, and who knows how they ended up in Maine and I got left behind. Can't be a practicing Muslim when you're five. Bad joke.

My "bio dad" and "bio mom," as my older son would say if he were with me. Glad he wasn't here tonight. I didn't want to scare him crapless. *Here, son. Take a look at this picture your daddy's friend bought for a song... it's going to fetch a hefty price if you can LOOK AT IT before we resell it. No way. DON'T LOOK. I love you, son.*

I loved it – the business of antiques – then we get stuff like THIS? A lithograph, they call it.

Li-tho-graph.

Mom and Dad didn't object when I dated and became engaged to Alice even though they were Episcopalians and Alice was an Italian Roman Catholic. What if Alice had been Muslim? I wondered about that. Is that why Dan and Mel sabotaged the friendship? Because I'm Arabic?

Strange thoughts began coursing through my mind, and I decided the isolation with the print was playing games with my mental health. I'm glad natural siblings came after me. Jerry and Siobhan, I love you. I'd be lost without you. They anchored me and let me know I had the right parents pick me. DON'T LOOK at the print, Jerry and Siobhan. Please.

There we go again with my strange thoughts.

Focus.

I have to try to sleep. Good sleep, unlike last night with the sound of mice under the parental summer house: the unfinished basement, which I'd dreaded even as a hefty teen. Didn't know there were critters down there. Pay the rent, critters. Where the hell was I going to put this thing – this li-tho-graph? Maybe the mice could eat it? Put some food on it. Maybe a nice chunk of cheddar. No government cheese for these mice. Hey, that's an idea. The mice could live in the house if they ate this lithograph. *Pay the rent, critters. EAT this print.*

Focus, you fuck. I looked at it again, and now the couple with no eyes had changed. They looked tanned like me. As a matter of fact, their hair changed in color too. Their hair was now deep dark brown, almost black. The woman was wearing a headscarf. There was a name for that. It just dawned on me that I'd never been there. Syria. Damascus, Syria. Way before Aleppo came on the map. There was unrest before Aleppo. The houses: made of clay and mud and the mosaics that were so stunningly detailed on the walls that curve to the ceilings of the mosques. I heard it's beautiful. Water fountains, dromedaries...

Dates!

Creepy. What just happened?

The background changed right before my eyes. That was no castle now. It was like the buildings you see in Morocco. With the minarets. Wait, no. It couldn't be. The couple in the foreground was definitely Arabic. What happened to the girl in the swing? *Okay, cool it, Sam the man. Get yourself a cheap dinner and relax, ex-lax. Just get one foot in front of the other on the carpet stained with green grass... and go... walk out. Don't look at the li-thograph. Run.* I'm so confused.

CHAPTER 28

The drive to Burger King didn't take long. Stress makes me hungry. It wouldn't take long with my heavy gas foot, trying to put as much distance as possible between me and that creepy print. The road had been desolate as I made my way down the hill, but the town center just a few miles away exuded some semblance of life. There it was, bright as my headlights.

As I turned the car into the large parking lot of the strip mall, relieved to be near civilization, I had a sudden change of heart and decided on fried whole clams instead. I steered out of the lot, turned back onto Elm and drove the extra three miles to the Lobster Catch Diner. I breathed a sigh, which told me I was relieved to be away from the dreadful print in that dreadful house, in that dreadful...

Stop it.

Focus.

No more strange thoughts.

My stomach was gurgling by the time I pulled into the Lobster Catch. It was close to 9 p.m. Right next to the –

It was closed.

I needed seafood. Seafood and eat it. Get it? Sea food. I am so flaming starved that my duck boots reminded me of the Peking duck we'd bought in New York's Chinatown this past summer. The kids loved it. Away from the parental summer home with the mice in the basement. Pay the rent, eat the print, or I'll give you government cheese.

Focus.

There was another restaurant somewhere. Jimmie's Clams. That's it. *Just keep driving and get a meal before you go stir-crazy, Sam.*

You wanted clams, you're going to get clams. Then you're heading back to the parental summer home even though you don't want to be there ever again, and stay the night. Don't mind the critters in the basement. They're there to eat the print. Okay?

Gas foot.

Turn here.

You have reached your destination.

I switched off the engine by the streetlight curbside and leaned back.

The comforting lights of Jimmie's. Still full of people.

I closed my eyes.

Relief.

It dawned with keen awareness...

I was afraid of being alone.

When did that happen?

Check on Alice's bottle of holy water from Lourdes. Where, oh where did I... Then I looked down.

A piece of paper was stuck on the bottom of my shoe.

Fuck this.

Don't tell me.

Yes, the print was stuck on the bottom of my foot, over the gas pedal. I reached down, snatching it. Then I flipped it over and realized it was an ad for someone's political campaign. I sighed. Getting jumpy, Sam. Too jumpy.

Into the bright lights and scents of New England comfort food. I sat people-watching after I ordered what must be the largest whole fried clam platter complete with extra tartar sauce and a side of... and that was when I saw it on the wall. A very similar print. I almost knocked over the gin and tonic I ordered as I strode over to a table by a wall. I stood almost over the couple, who were minding their own privacy as I examined the picture. It wasn't a lithograph, but the background and foreground were the same: the castle with turrets and red pennants in the background and the girl on a swing, in the act of swinging. Quickly, I reached into my pocket for my iPhone and took a picture. I looked around, realized the couple was looking up at me, and apologized, explaining my interest in the shot. The guy actually stood up, wiped his beard with a napkin, and offered for me to get closer. "No, I'm good now. Sorry again."

I walked away and flagged the waitress and asked if she knew who provided the framed photo on the wall, pointing it out, as there were others.

"No, but the owner is here tonight. Would you like me to ask him to come to your table?"

"Please."

CHAPTER 29

I t was close to eleven p.m. by the time I coasted the Volvo back onto the driveway of my parents' summer house. I had forgotten, in my haste to leave, to turn even one light on, so I was in darkness.

The headlights cast an ethereal glow over the front stairs of the house leading to the expansive porch. The front door looked forlorn and so did the dark sightless windows. Like the sightless couple who stared back at me from the lithograph print.

I was afraid to shut off the engine, but I did. Still seated, I pulled out my cell phone to examine the picture from the restaurant with the help of the driver's side vanity mirror. There it was: the photo I'd snapped of the picture back at the restaurant. I sat there totally dumbfounded. It wasn't the same as my print. Fuck.

I must've taken a shot of the wrong print. I must've looked ridiculous, even inebriated. But I knew what I'd seen. I saw the same picture, the same exact one as the lithograph, li-tho-graph, just inside the house here. Maybe that was why I got a free dinner. The owner of the restaurant looked suspiciously at me, looked again at the picture on the wall, asked the couple to "please don't mind us," and looked again at my iPhone shot. "What castle?" he said. "I don't see a girl," he said. Same shot, same lighting. No castle, no turrets, no flags or a girl on a swing. He showed me my own iPhone. "Yours also shows the guitar guy," he said.

So now I looked again, seated in my Volvo with the Bluetooth and the eight-speaker system from Bose, perspiring in my armpits, and the heat wasn't even on. I was looking at a man who held a guitar, a classical guitar, in his forties, grinning at the camera. A local musician with the name of Rodrigo something something who played a gig just a few months ago. No girl, no swing, no castle. Just Rodrigo. I kept examining my iPhone, and it didn't change, even after I put it down and then put in the password to unlock the phone again. Nope. Nothing like the dratted lithograph.

I remembered how I quickly ate my dinner when it came, served by a frumpy-looking waitress. It had looked so good when I ordered it, and when I got it, I ate it for the sake of eating it. Extra tartar sauce? Yes. Cocktail? No. Who cares? Meanwhile, as I ate, I kept staring at the framed picture on the wall of – Rodrigo the guitarist. The couple finally left, self-consciously, I might add. Here's NOT looking at you, kid. Later the owner returned to my table with a look that said pity all over it and told me the meal was on the house and good luck with my cell phone. He seemed to want as much distance from me as Dan, my former friend, did.

Fuck you, Dan.

I am outta here. Tonight. I hit the speed dial, and Alice's sleepy voice came on.

"Hey, what's going on? Are you staying?"

Silence. I was deliberating, as I couldn't find her holy water.

"Yeah."

"What happened? Did you burn it?"

"I'm burying it again. I need holy water."

"I gave you the one from Lourdes."

"I think it might be in the house there somewhere."

"You left it here?"

"It's not up here."

Silence. She had put the phone down.

Minutes pass.

"The holy water's here. Just put that print back in the ground... or burn it."

"I tried. It's not even scorched."

Silence. Did I just shock you, Alice, or are you thinking?

"Hon?"

"Come home and get the holy water, dear."

"I'll bury it again."

"But leave it alone this time."

"IF it stays buried."

She yawned, and I knew she was tired.

"So what are you doing? Are you headed home? It's kinda late."

"I guess I'm staying."

"If you are, the priest here said to put it in sacred ground if you can't put holy water on it. I don't want it in our parish, so bury it at a church there."

"What?! Sacred... what?!"

CHAPTER 30

The mice kept me up. Scratching the floorboards, the walls, even moving the lithograph. I turned it upside down on the kitchen counter and put some moldy cheese from the refrigerator on it. Was it Brie or Chevre? STOP the tangential thoughts. I woke up to find the cheese gone, but the picture – they didn't even pee on it. Pay the rent. Pee on the dratted print.

This time, I didn't turn it over. No way.

I checked my cell phone, though. It was still Rodrigo the guitar player.

I googled "sacred ground" and drove to the local church. I dashed out of the Volvo and aimed for the rectory, but a man who appeared to be the groundskeeper blocked me as I darted for the building's entrance. He indicated that the priest was very busy with masses, as it was a Sunday. Good. I wasn't sure how I was going to explain myself. He'd just given me time.

I sat in the Volvo as the man walked away. How was I to explain that my wife told me that an antique picture was haunted because some people, my best friend for one, me for another, had seen some strange changes in a picture. Then I had to explain that he, the priest, had to bless it and bury it in the churchyard or someplace considered "sacred ground." Alice, always pragmatic, logical and more levelheaded than me, had consulted with our parish priest, who insisted upon it. She'd told the monsignor it had made me "unstable" and too, too stressed. It was doing something to me. I was hallucinating, or Dan, Mel and I were all collectively hallucinating.

"No," Alice said. "Not hallucinating. The lithograph is 'cursed.'" Her word, not mine, or maybe it was the monsignor's. "It's feeding on your emotions and making changes as you think," she explained after I told her what and how it changed according to my thoughts. How it didn't rot even when I'd put it in the ground weeks ago. *Do you want to see it, Alice? No. Just joking.* "Bless it and keep it buried up there." *Yes, Alice.* "Come home, Sam. The store needs tending." *Yes, Alice.* "More antiques are coming." Of course they were. Okay, but let me resolve this. "No more cursed antiques, please." *How am I supposed to know that, dear? Just kidding. Poor joke. Poor me.*

Should I tell the priest all that?

Then, minutes before I drove to the church, Alice called: "Hi, hon. I have news for you."

I flurried my hair with my fingers. "Tell me you have a solution, dear."

I could hear Alice sigh. "I finally got Mel."

They'd sort of made up and arranged to "do lunch" the following week. Alice had to beg. Meanwhile, Alice wanted to know what Mel had seen. Mel got emotional. She saw her first baby in the picture, who'd passed away from a lung infection the pediatrician had failed to diagnose at age four. It was swinging on the swing like a grown child, except she was only four. How the heck could a lithograph know about something that was the lowest point in her life? How cruel and evil.

Dan saw, after thinking about his brother, a man who looked

a lot like him standing like the soldier that he had been before he was gunned down during a tour of duty in Afghanistan. The same swarthy complexion, same uniform, same smile. And they were both thinking avidly about these beautiful people in their lives before looking at the lithograph in the living room – in a frame, ready to sell.

Ready to sell to an unsuspecting customer – to pass on to me IF it didn't sell. Then I was going to give it back, and they wouldn't even come down the driveway. "Let's keep in touch by phone. We don't want it to stick to us." It?

"Alice," I said, "please. They're not friends. Don't have lunch with her anymore."

Alice paused. The line, I thought, went dead.

"Okay, I'll text her and cancel."

I felt better after hearing that. After hearing that whatever we were thinking imprinted on the print, and it wasn't just me. It wasn't just our family – you, Mom and Dad. Shit. I wasn't crazy or losing it. It fed on what I was thinking or who I was thinking about. That was pretty profound. AND that friendship was OVER. I just realized as I sat there what I had back there at that summer house.

That call from Mel that morning finally gave me the impetus I needed. So here I was, entering a stranger's church in a town I dreaded, to talk to a priest I'd never met. Did my parents tithe? Oh shit. It was Roman Catholic. I hoped Brock or Bill or Bob didn't walk out as I walked in. Would they let me in, as I was Arabic? *It's Maine, people.*

Here goes. Focus.

The heavy oak door latched shut. In the coolness of the narthex I waited until all the parishioners left, then walked up to the priest. He turned to me in his robe and stole with a gaze like I was a penitent asking forgiveness from Jesus Christ. Actually, I felt I needed Jesus Christ.

I told Father what's-his-name everything. From acquisition, to attempted sale, to the two friends – how it came to be in our house and what had happened to my parents when they saw what they saw. *Did you get that all down, Father?* Then I came back and dug it up after I dreamed it was in our bedroom or thought I saw it on the floor of our bedroom. Remember how Alice saw it hanging in the drawing room? When in fact I had taken it to the store? So I took it up here. Then I had a nightmare that it wasn't decaying... blah, blah, blah. Then the conversations Mel had with said friends and what our own priest said to do. I caught myself repeating myself.

I was now thinking in circles.

Boy, the priest was looking at me real funny. *Sorry, Father, I'm probably the first Muslim on sacred ground you've ever met. More fun than I thought. I'm being sarcastic.*

He seemed furious. In retrospect, I think he was furious at his own inability to help. "Why didn't you just return it?" he asked, cleric collar all starched and white.

"They wouldn't take it."

"You can't sell something strange like that."

"We didn't. We couldn't."

"Of course not, Sam... it's Sam, right?"

"Yes. Sam. It scared people. My wife's friend finally told us everything."

"Yes, you already told me that."

"Dan gave it to me instead."

"You said that already. Why didn't you keep it buried?"

"It didn't stay buried, but it was, so I discovered, when I got up to the summer house."

The priest rolled his eyes.

I continued babbling: "Then I was having nightmares that it wasn't rotting like it was supposed to. Like my parents are rotting, like the summer house is rotting, like our pets when they're not cremated are rotting."

The priest looked at me, totally baffled.

"Yes, Father, I am as confused as you."

He paused, looked away, then looked back at me. I had grown agitated.

"Well, you were afraid, and now your fears have conjured your worst expectation," he said.

"What's that supposed to mean, Father? I hoped it wasn't rotting?"

"You FEARED it wasn't rotting, and it answered your fear."

"Shit."

"Don't curse, please."

"What do I do now?"

"Let me see... How has this print changed your life?"

"You really wanna know?"

"You lost friends?"

"Yes."

"Your marriage?"

"Not yet."

"Customers?"

"Yes."

"Anything else?"

"I need my sanity back."

When I said that, the man seemed to relax. Yeah. He knew. "May I see it, please?"

"It's at my parents' house. Will you come with me?"

The man studied me for a few minutes, then appeared lost in thought. I think he was trying to figure out if it was safe to go with me. "No, I just want to see it. You may bring it here."

CHAPTER 31

No sacred ground. The priest took one look and blessed the lithograph, making the sign of the cross. It was the original scene he saw: the castle and the swing with the girl. With resolve, he handed it back to me with a flourish, as if humoring me. I felt like a child. So I stood my ground and refused to leave the chapel unless he took a long look at it. It was already late in the afternoon.

"Young man, if it would make you feel better, leave it here on this pew overnight. Come back next morning, and if it hasn't changed as you say it does, take it. I blessed it."

"No, it only changes when you think about something or someone."

The man stared at me for the longest time. "Where did it come from?"

"It was at an auction in New York." I paused, not ready to tell him it originated somewhere in the Middle East. Something about his vibe told me to hold off this time.

"Why was it auctioned, do you know?"

"No, I'm afraid not. Antiques get auctioned all the time for various reasons."

"Some things are better left alone."

"Should I just toss it in the trash? I need to be back at the store tomorrow morning. It's Monday."

"I'm not telling you anything of that sort. If this is like a Ouija board, and I'm in no way an expert, you shouldn't tear it up when you toss it."

Well, priest man, it won't tear anyway, but I won't tell you that either, I thought. "Then what are you telling me, Father?"

"Leave it here tonight, as I said. I will look at it tonight and give it back to you with some ideas in the morning."

"Okay. I guess I'll have to stay one more night to resolve this."

I made a move to leave, then hesitated. "Father?"

"Yes?" This said with an impatient tone.

"Has anyone ever encountered anything like this in your experience?"

He looked away, examining the baptismal font in the adjacent chapel as if it was going to give him an answer. "No, but there is a woman who is better able to advise you on this. She believes in something called psychic photography, which seems similar to what you are claiming here."

"Can you tell me her contact information?"

He touched the crucifix on his chest as he fumbled for a reply. "I am a Roman Catholic priest. I am not recommending you connect with her, but since you seem at a loss, I can give you her number. She's close by."

"Do you believe me?"

"It's what you believe and experience that matters. I hope you're not dabbling in the occult. That would open up all kinds of things you will not be able to close."

"Trust me, I am not. I just need to ask her what needs to be done."

"Okay. Don't tell her I sent you. I will pray tonight for an answer." He examined me. "Sam, do you believe in God?"

"I do."

With that, he extended a wiry hand, and I handed him the lithograph. He dismissively placed it on a pew with a prayer book on top to secure it.

CHAPTER 32

The answer to the prayer came. I think. The lithograph sat in the pew of the church overnight and didn't change. According to the priest, anyway. He handed me a phone number and a vial of holy water.

A study with a bunch of roses in assorted vases, a huge bay window with lace curtains. A large reddish leather sofa with two matching armchairs faced a square coffee table that looked really expensive. Huge Etruscan figureheads sat on the coffee table. In the middle of this was a small mahogany cafe-style table with four mahogany chairs, late eighteenth century, from what I could surmise. In this arrangement, we sat facing each other. The woman, Erica, appeared to be an antique collector of sorts. She also liked art, contemporary, it appeared, from the contrasting acrylic canvases on the walls of the room. It gave the expansive room a very eclectic vibe, which was comforting. Expressive, warm and definitely cultured. The rest of the room had all sorts of books. It added to the aura of a highly refined woman of means.

She examined the print with a blank look on her features.

"The process does not work with a lithograph. Only film photographs."

"I see."

"Are you familiar with how lithographs are made? It works very differently from film developing..."

I studied the woman in her fifties, her hair in a ponytail, her body lean and in a jogging outfit with "Adidas" printed on the spandex. She looked nothing like I would imagine a psychic or someone interested in mysticism.

I envisioned the prototypical heavyset woman in a gypsy outfit. I guess I was biased. Like I am a Muslim without the requisite headgear. Or beard. I don't even eat Indian food. So there. *Focus. You're a racist, Sam. A profiler against your own race. Focus.* She looked more like a girl you'd encounter in a public park while you were walking your dog, and you thought she was cute. She was cute in her own way, but I was more concerned about getting the print out of my life.

I had to tell her how I got her contact information, contrary to the priest's request. The priest hadn't seen anything change in the morning when he picked it up from the pew, but did notice it was frayed at the edges, like it got wet or mildewed. I never did figure out why that happened. I begged him to keep it there until it finally deteriorated and the images were worn like an old photograph. I told her that. He told me if she had no ideas, as a last resort to bring it back.

"Okay, then if it isn't a psychic photo, then what is it?"

She looked away and pointed out another photo on her wall, framed in a cream and gold frame. It was different from the rest, as it added a personal touch to the room. A boy about seven in overalls, holding a baby calf.

"That's my brother, who was a twin."

"Was?"

"I miss him a lot."

"What happened to him?"

Instead of answering me, she shut her eyes as she placed one hand on top of my lithograph, which lay upside down on the cafe table.

Minutes went by, and I finally sighed and looked around the opulent room, part of me wishing I lived there.

Then Erica opened her eyes and turned the lithograph over.

She looked down at the lithograph, and then I knew what she was hoping to see.

She moved the print towards me and turned it so the subject faced me.

It was the same scene: the castle and the girl on the swing.

She cleared her throat. "I think this only responds to you."

"It changed for my friends. I don't understand it."

"I'm sorry if I don't have an answer. I will need to do some research."

"What do I do meanwhile? I can't bring it back to the store... word was going around..."

"Just put it in storage. Under lock and key."

I realized then that I had somehow become obsessed with the print. Like a kid with a Facebook page, I had to keep looking at it. I had to tell her. I didn't know what else to do.

"It needs you, or you need it for some reason."

"But why? My friend and his wife were able to let go... to hand it to me and not turn back..."

"Because it has a hold on you, and you're allowing it."

I looked down at the print. I gasped.

The castle in the background was gone. In its place was a large house – or was a house – which had turned into a wreck. Debris, a charred roof with a gaping hole, and windows all burned and blown out. In the foreground, the remains of what appeared to be a burned sedan.

I must have been holding my breath.

Erica was watching my reaction and moved the print towards her. Her eyes were mirroring mine as she studied it.

"My brother died in a house fire. A gas explosion from a propane tank."

We both looked at each other and examined it. Her reaction told me we were seeing the same scene. Here, now, in her study. I finally had the validation I needed in real time.

Unlike me, she didn't look surprised. I was, however, aghast.

The mice finally paid the rent.

I stood up in her beautiful study with the sunlight streaming through the lace curtain windows. My breath came in expansive gasps like I had been underwater and now had surfaced. Pools of clarity washed over me. "I see."

She nodded without expression, as if stifling an emotion. However, I could feel the emotion despite her stoic expression.

She handed me back the lithograph. "It reads the past. Whoever has the strongest emotion imprints on it."

"Any memory with a strong feeling."

She looked away. "From the past."

Erica looked out the window, past me, past the antique furniture.

She picked it up. "Come."

She led me out of the room, which I then realized was a home office of sorts, judging from some nearby file cabinets and a blotter situated on a nearby desk. We walked past a large family room and into a large kitchen; then we ascended to the second floor. At the landing of the stairs, I saw that we were on an internal balcony of sorts where there was a commanding view of the backyard with children's swings on the lawn, then a swimming pool with hedges on two sides. Again, a very opulent space. Yet, amidst all this success, she was down-to-earth, approachable.

Erica nudged me on the shoulder to awaken my reverie, lost

in the beauty that was her home. I realized that the validation from a stranger who had no interest other than to solve my dilemma had given me space to admire and to see things I had ignored before.

"Over here," she said.

We walked down the hall and entered a room lined with bookcases from top to bottom – the middle opened to the study below that we were just in. We were on the second floor of the study library, and above me was a third level, which appeared to be a stone turret with windows on four sides. On either side of each window were more bookcases. Above the bookcases, at eye level, were small paintings on the walls.

She turned. "How much do you want for it?"

I was taken aback.

"I'm serious."

"Of course I want to get rid of it."

"This is your opportunity."

"You're sure."

"My husband was a museum curator. This is very rare."

"Rare, but..."

"He has heard of these types of artifacts... on trips to the Middle East."

"So you know where it came from. How much do you think it's worth?"

"How much was Dan trying to sell it for?"

Silence. I was perplexed.

"I never told you my friend's name," I replied.

CHAPTER 33

We climbed an internal stair to the turret. There, Erica pulled a frame off the wall and proceeded to remove a print from the frame. I noticed the frame was double glazed. Thick glass.

I handed her back the lithograph.

"I have holy water," I offered.

"I have one too. Blessed from Jerusalem."

From a nearby bookshelf, she reached for a small bottle and uncapped it.

She turned the print over on a table, the scene downwards.

Four sides she blessed and then the center with the mark of a cross.

The double-glazed frame fitted perfectly like it was meant for it.

Then she positioned the frame and hung it. "It needed a home, but not one where it's visible to anyone who may not be ready for it."

"I see."

"Your friends were not ready for it, and neither were you. I think you were fascinated to own something so unusual, to say the least, so you couldn't let go. It's Middle Eastern, so perhaps your friends thought you were a fit, as your ancestry... "

"My birth parents were from Damascus."

Erica gave me a knowing look. "Have you ever heard of a djinn? It can play with your mind and manipulate your emotions. Very dangerous."

I surveyed the turret. "But up here..."

"Up here someone has to climb up on purpose to view it. I would be the only one at this point who may see the past in it as you have."

"At an obscure location where children..."

"Or other adults would not be able to see it."

"Will you let me know if anything happens?"

"I will keep in touch. But as long as the glass holds and it's blessed, we should be good."

It's now 2020. I have not heard from Erica since then. Months later, Alice and I did a final tag sale on my parents' summer house. I sprinkled the holy water from Lourdes around the house before I finally sold it, convinced that the lithograph had finally found a home.

Since then we've sold several antiques of every imaginable sort and expanded to a larger store. Alice remained friends with Mel, though it's now casual. My associate Dan laid low until one summer when he offered me an antique chest to see if it could be sold in my new store. I declined, now reluctant to take anything from him.

I never went back to the Bar Harbor area or to Erica's town, where her home with a turret houses a print that was mine. When I look back and recall the scene in that lithograph, I now realize that the girl on the swing looked a lot like Erica, as much as the castle in the foreground looked a lot like her home.

It all came into focus.

PART IV

THE FURNITURE ROOM

CHAPTER 34

VALENTINA

The scent of lavender always lingers in my head like a memory of a lover. It stays and stays in your mind even when the clothes have been sent away to be washed and pressed. Sheets sit in the sun, drying and then starched, and like lovers' scents willfully purified; but the elusive scent of lavender, though gentle, remains long after a lover has been dead. That's just the way lavender is. However, unlike a lover, which brings about a frisson of shame, lavender is clean, lighter and is a chiaroscuro of blue and purple in the Mediterranean sun. For me, the memory of lavender remains as that scent of purity and not the texture or thrill of a lover's skin. That cleanliness is like no other, like a wash day in the old home of my childhood in Spain: in Garabandal, just several breathing steps from the lady apparition that became world famous.

But lavender was made even more memorable, as my mother wore lavender on her pinafore and thrice-hemmed house dress. My memories are etched indelibly by scents. Her sepia photo hangs framed in the front room of my apartment in Bergerac, facing the vineyards beyond: it shows her standing in the parlor of our humble stone and thatch two-room house in humble and rural Garabandal. When I look at that photo, I smell lavender, and my heart dances.

However, misfortune can strip us of our vivid memories of serenity, of joy – even the vivid scent of lavender and its purity – when sullied and maligned by fear. A harvest of fear that came about when Jacques and I chose to rent a particular store in Vermont. I attest to its truth, over my father's tomb. It is as true as the apparition of Garabandal. As you can tell, I am about remembrance now that I'm old. It's how beauty stays in my memory – and how the unquiet and haunted marred that beauty.

It began with a move to that antique store in Vermont, which I will keep unnamed. Even though I shiver up to now, I cringe to remember exactly what I smelled and heard that day like it was just yesterday, but cringe I must so I can tell you all the details.

When I heard you were coming to visit once again and wanted the story of my halcyon days when I lived in New England and ran a haunted shop, I was torn. First, a gripping dream overwhelmed me that I was back there again, transported to that street of warehouses and tradespeople milling about. Then I realized I had to purge my thoughts and feelings in order to reclaim my serenity when I thought of my mother and the days of innocence, my childhood and the lavender that grew so freely.

I heard you may be in Perigueux. We can talk about the haunted store if you want to get some Mexican food, as there is one there. I would love to join you, as I do have a predilection for anything that reminds me of Spanish cuisine, as you know I am Cantabrian, and I know your grandmother was Castilian. We have a lot in common, more than you think. But on the off chance that the pandemic interferes with your plans once again to get to this side of paradise, I thought I'd write to you.

I hope you don't mind that my writing is fragmented as

much as my memories have come to be. I decided it was probably better than to wait to see you in person to get all the details down lest I forget – and Jacques takes me to the *medecin* (doctor) again for the back problem I have encountered. It would be terrible to not meet up or share the story I've been waiting to tell you in great detail. Here then, is my story, and you can best see fit which parts to submit and perhaps, if too wordy, I don't mind a few deletions, but it's pretty accurate considering. Please kindly include my introduction here.

CHAPTER 35

I began my story with the scent of lavender because that's the one that triggers the strongest memories of the apparitions, like the lady in Garabandal. Then I will tell you about the music I am familiar with, since this account of mine deals also with music and how that too was sullied by dread.

When I think of music, I think of the groups of my youth, like the Spanish bands that came to Santander: Los Brincos, Bruno Lomas and Los Pekenikes with the cute and slim guitarist. I used curlers on our hair, my sister and I, and we had it done every few weeks or sometimes every week in those days. I even think I liked British rock and even music like my former university friend used to dance to. I now forget his name. He was a gentleman like Esteban, a former lover, before I married Jacques.

However, the music I heard in the antique shop was nothing like the ones I liked – all I remember is that when I heard it, it made tendrils of cold drafts down my back, and the melody filled me with despair and dread. To this day I cannot place the era, the singer nor the musical instrument, which sounded a cross between a flute and a type of harpsichord. Perhaps if you visit the shop in Vermont and were unfortunate enough to enter the back room, you may identify it. I counsel you against it.

The lavender is related to the music in that haunted place and the scent of old wood, which is common in antique stores and homes with antique furniture. The shop in Vermont was much that way, with that combination of scents: wood that is moldy and with dust motes that flecked in the sunbeams from windows. Then, when things really got strange and sinister – the scent of sulfur arrives like a scorpion – it strikes the unsuspecting. Have you been burning candles? Lighting them in the store? Jacques would ask.

The shop in Vermont left me a fearful woman even still in my fifties. Now when I enter a shop, even a cheese shop or a butcher's for sausages, I still tremble when I smell something that seems like the old wood of that shop in Vermont, some perfume that is lavender, or when a match is lit. Then I shiver because that haunting melody plays in my head. It's quite painful for me to recall them, but since I consider this an exercise in letting go of a creepy memory, a month of nightmares for both me and the old husband, I have decided to write it all. Jacques thinks it may actually be therapeutic. After all, we're now well away from Vermont and the world of antiques, save for the old ballet shoes that I used to collect, but I know who owns them. The music from the shop destroyed my vivid memories of the bands from my youth because it conjures them. I can almost hear you say it's not fair. The shop robbed you of the pleasure of music and the scents of your youth.

So many triggers that left me unsettled.

I'm not sure why I didn't make note of it that summer when we decided we would move to a much larger store at the far end of town. First of all, the new store wasn't a store situated where the old little store had been, nestled in the middle of the antique row. This store was much bigger, but it was near the warehouses and off in a more remote section. That in itself worried me. People are used to walking in the antique area for antiques, taking in a coffee or ice-cream cone nearby and then strolling to the restaurants in the next block. This store, well, it was farther afield. A short drive, almost, especially for the older patrons who can't walk as much anymore. It was surrounded by tailoring and tools shops, odds and ends of more the likes of welders and plumbers. Then there were the warehouses and the buildings that were turned into some type of apartments for the young, which looked industrial inside and outside. These large apartments later on became more suitable for the well-to-do, as they were quite high-end. No university pupils could afford them, and neither can people in their twenties when their careers just began.

However, the larger store was reasonable as far as the rent. I think that is ultimately why we considered it and signed the lease after a few visits. I remember after Jacques signed it that I kept asking if it was okay that it wasn't anywhere near an antique row. It ate at me, and I think my gut was telling me something was not right. There was a penumbra of foreboding that left me repelled from packing. I wanted to stay at the old store. Jacques allayed my fears as much as Esteban would have. He said that was okay, as we were advertising everywhere, even in auctions, where we were moving and when. Our faithful clients would follow us, and the tourists who relished vintage would as well. It wasn't like it was a completely different town or state. It was just a very short drive. Closer than Santander was to Garabandal.

But you see, Garabandal was sacred. It was a Holy Virgin apparition.

This one, though also about apparitions, sounds and scents, wasn't sacred.

I didn't know anything about the building except that it

seemed odd, sitting there like a big brownstone in the middle of warehouses. There were garages where you can have your car or truck serviced, there were fish canneries, even, but no other apartment building like this one, which it looked to be at one time. Then someone told me someone rented out flats there before it was demolished and renovated to make it so every floor looked clean and airy. To make room for offices and stores. Ours was going to be a store with a second floor. It was, in fact, the largest of the offices, with one massive walk-up entrance of double doors made of heavy wood like you would see in a church door. Then, the inside was very vintage. Like me. Old. There were tin ceilings like in the 1930s, which reminded me of the gangster movies. The dark wood paneling. I liked paneling. But this one, it made the rooms of the store dark. Too dark, in fact. The chandeliers and sconces on the walls made up for the darkness in some spaces, lighting it up like a dance hall. They were the original chandeliers and sconces, moved here and there to accommodate the renovations when walls were knocked down.

Some needed cleaning, from what I recall, and I asked the building owner if that was possible before we moved in. His reply was very telling at the time, but we, eager beavers that we were, didn't pay much attention to his reply. He said: "I will try to get a cleaning crew, but it's difficult to enlist them these days, as they have to come at nighttime. Nighttime is a problem for them." What that meant, I guess we now know. I thought it was odd, as most cleaning people in offices and stores DO come after office hours and into the night. I can't imagine them cleaning while the store was open. Can you?

CHAPTER 36

When every piece of antique had been moved, it was smaller than we thought. The space was double the size of the old store, but we both underestimated how much we had acquired through estate sales, pickers who bought from salvaging heirloom things from old homes, couples who restored and renovated and had no place for a piece of furniture... and the fellow dealer eager to barter an object for another. Plus, of course, the third-party consignment vendors. We had to give them a few feet of space for their vintage wares.

In those days, we examined every lamp, porcelain, and knickknack for flaws and authenticity. The larger items we looked for any type of flaw that would signal a cheaper sale or even, perhaps, an exquisitely made fake.

By the time we were done and moved in, it was almost four months later, and the leaves of fall came sailing past windows and into open doors. The early darkness came with it, and the store's fixtures, especially the chandeliers, which were antique themselves, cast an eerie pallor on the vintage and antique objects we considered art forms of a bygone era. I wandered through this panoply of objects with customers and replied to questions of every type. Where did it come from, how old, can you measure it, does it come as a pair? Like that and this and that. But I'm moving too fast now.

Allow me to begin with day one: opening day. Opening day was slow but significant. That was the day when we received two vases and a chest.

One vase, a sizable one at two feet high, came with a twin. It was a large very ornate vase we'd grabbed from a shop in far-off northern Georgia, at the feet of the Soviet Republic. Between the two ornate affairs was a chest, which besotted Jacques as soon as he saw it at a fair. Somehow, it reminded him of a French hope chest. But it came from a Spanish galleon, according to the picker, who served time on board a ship. We placed the chest, quite a heavy one with straps and a bolt, between the two vases and called it a day. I just remember them distinctly more than others, as they will figure later in my story. Hold on to that and remember this chest.

The next day, a Monday, my store manager, Meg, a lithe woman with a face showing lines of worry, came in early, as it was her first day at the new location. I had given her the combination to the alarm and the key to the interior door, though we didn't set the alarm. I think in the hustle and bustle, we forgot to set it. She switched the light on at the entrance door, one hand on the handle of her Hermes bag (as she was trying to impress us with her visits to the French Luberon) and one holding her Starbucks cup with the key dangling from her wrist.

The delicate but unmistakable scent of lavender filled her nostrils and overpowered her latte. She thought it strange, but since she was prone to fantasy, her retelling initially told us she was a romantic. That was our interpretation at the time. She wore perfume herself, and since she was a collector of French perfume, much cheaper to procure than what we had at the old store, I assumed she was daydreaming the scent from a bygone trip she had taken recently. It didn't stop there, however. Meg stood stupefied, nevertheless. She recounted wondering as she stood there if I had just preceded her in arriving, as it was the first week of opening. It was logical, she pondered, that I took it upon myself to open and be there ahead of her on Sunday. Remember, while she was closing shop at the old store, I had been there on opening day, Friday.

Meg stepped into the shop in that light-footed way of hers with her museum of art umbrella and placed it on the stand near the entrance. She called out my name several times, but there was no reply. She recalls later forgetting the umbrella as she dashed past it into the open rain. Her heeled shoes made soft clicking sounds, and as she proceeded deeper into the shop, the lavender scent disappeared. Meg called out to me again and again since she sensed a presence, still sniffing for the waft of lavender that she elucidated signaled my perfumed presence. I never wore lavender. I loved the scent, but it didn't become me, and now you know I never would, as it conjures bad memories.

As the scent had dissipated, she wandered, still searching for me in the store, and eventually strode to the back counter where the register was located. She then realized she was alone and felt a sense of loneliness upon surmising no one was in the store but her. Meg never felt lonely, being a child in a family of six.

A slave to routine, Meg did what she did at the beginning of every shift. She perused the ledger of the day before, opened a new sales ledger for the new day, and proceeded to check the list of deliveries and listed items that were reserved for customer transport or pickup. The miscellaneous and boring things you don't think about that make up an antique store. Visa, Amex, Mastercard or Discover. She was just about to step into the ladies' room, as the coffee had made it past her gut, when the scent of lavender returned, this time with a vengeance.

Meg decided she would investigate, as she claimed it seemed the scent came from a candle. Meg had the unfortunate incident as a child of having to dash out of a burning house when her grandmother forgot to snuff out a candle that caught fire. As a young woman, she was now cautious, and we were glad for that.

Please allow me to explain how the new store was set up: When Jacques and I placed items in the new store, we decided we would make it as inviting as possible by not cluttering the front windows, but placing some antique paintings and statues on display to entice others to come inside. Through the entrance door, we placed a runner in a muted blue floral pattern, allowing for a small foyer for people to temporarily stand and pause, taking in the breadth of the large shop. We found that when customers were not overwhelmed by clutter upon entering, they relaxed and stayed longer, as the atmosphere exuded comfort and style.

As the customer walked down the runner, a series of small antique jewelry in display cases welcomed the customer to their right and left, which was more like a setup at a department store that sold makeup and jewelry. Some contemporary chairs were positioned so that if they chose to hang there to examine some period pieces, they could sit while the shop seller showed them the piece of interest. That shop seller would be either me or Meg. Later on, we set up a coffee and tea butler there with cream and sugars.

Meg walked out from behind one of these counters, where she had assembled the ledgers behind the jewelry, and sauntered down the length of the runner into the four sections of the store. It was an idea I had of sectioning the antique china in a separate area from the statues and religious icons on the left, and then across the aisle was the heavy furniture and finally the smaller miscellaneous pieces to the right. She walked into the china section and found the scent less pronounced. She then entered the statues and icon section and found them as usual.

It was when Meg crossed to the threshold of the back area, where the large furniture was laid out, that she felt a distinctive sense of foreboding. This section was physically farther than the rest of the four rooms, as there was a small stair that led down to it. A room that was lower than the rest. It was also where the large twin vases and the chest from the Spanish galleon also found a temporary home until a buyer bought them.

Meg wandered into the area where the chest and vases sat, touched them to decide whether they needed dusting, then content they did not, she stepped away and looked out the window, which was her habit. She surveyed the crowded room piled with all types of period furniture and decided there were no candles there or even incense sticks, which I do not have use for and never found attractive. Cautious as ever, Meg was.

The back of the store looked out onto a narrow alley where the brick buildings sat side by side. After studying the alley for people or passersby, she decided to return to the counter towards the front of the store. Upon turning, she thought that someone had entered the shop, as a draft blew on the nape of her neck.

She stepped up a few steps and out of the room to check. That's when she felt something following behind her, though there were no footsteps. Meg turned back, a cold draft wafting across her face. Of course, there was no one there. The room was empty. Discomfited by the experience, Meg called me, I think, just to hear another voice.

"I'm stepping out for lunch. So far, everything has been quiet."

"Good. Get something to eat before you wither." I laughed. I always taunted Meg about her weight, which was on the thin side.

"I'm going to the deli. Would you like anything?"

Again, that question was out of character, as Meg never asked me about what we were doing for lunch.

"No, thank you. We're about finished here, and then we'll join you there. We just ate lunch." I had some last-minute details at the old store, which were items from a third-party vendor, Charley. He needed to transport his own antiques to the new location with the help of his son, who brought a truck. He had just loaded the last of the antiques after packing them onto the truck when Meg rang. Knowing Meg from several years of working side by side as our store manager, I sensed something afoot. Instead of addressing it on the phone, I refrained, as it was better discussed in person, which is my style.

CHAPTER 37

J acques had just pulled away from the curb, and we were en route with Charley following in their truck when Meg rang my mobile again.

"Sorry to bother you, Val. Were you just here or one of the vendors?" she asked.

"No. We're headed there now."

"Oh. The lights were off."

"You didn't turn them off before you left?"

"No, I didn't. I just put the sign on that we'd be back as usual at two and locked the door."

"Anything amiss?" I turned to Jacques, who was driving, wondering if someone broke in, but why bother with the lights?

"I will check now. The bolt was secure, but I didn't arm the alarm."

"Okay. We're headed over now, if you want to wait."

She waited. Meg appeared a bit edgy to me. She stood huddled under the awning by the front door with the keys in her hand. The rain had just stopped, but it was evident she had walked out without her umbrella.

We parked curbside and emerged, the weather still gloomy

as if the clouds had become too heavy to bear water. It appeared about to pour again.

I unlocked the door with Jacques behind me, turned all the lights back on – and the smell of lavender immediately met me. Meg wiped her shoes at the door and followed us in.

I turned, sniffing. "You're wearing...?"

"No, Val. But I know what you mean. I smelled lavender this morning as I came in."

Jacques proceeded to survey each room as we stood and opened the register. With few or no customers that day, there were no receipts. Meg checked the cash, and it was just as she'd left it.

Room to room we went and inspected. Everything was just as we had laid them out. Jacques checked against the photographs we take as a way of comparing against anything that might be missing. A vendor one time who brought their goods on consignment alleged there was an item, a lamp, unaccounted for. We learned to photograph often and date them.

The gloom descended, and the rain began again. Later that day, since there were no customers coming after five p.m., we closed earlier than usual, checking the windows in the back room where the alley was located, setting the alarms, which we'd neglected to do until that night. Feeling reassured that the alarm would go off and connect directly with the police, we left for the evening. Jacques noted that all the lights were off and the front door bolted and secure.

Weary and wet from the day though it was a few hours shorter than most days, Jacques and I retired early that evening, feeling that once customers had acclimated to our new location, we would have to put in longer hours like usual. It was not often that we had the luxury of a day like that day, and though Mondays were usually slow with customers, once the winter settled in, we began in earnest with contracting with new vendors, estate sales and auctions. With the summer closing and the new school year already beginning, the stores saw fewer tourists with their children and reverted back to the routines of old-timers and avid collectors who were more serious than the average tourist.

Other than the lights mysteriously shutting off when Meg had left to get lunch, Meg and I didn't notice anything unusual save for the lavender smell we detected upon entering. That eerie feeling of being followed, thank God, didn't stay with Meg. A brave woman used to adversity, she needed to patrol those rooms even after hours to tidy up and spot anything broken or amiss. She was a Godsend to us.

CHAPTER 38

The next morning, renewed and rested by a short day and an early night, I arrived and attempted to settle into the old routine in a new location. The month of November began, and as I expected, the customers who regularly prowled our aisles were more of the serious antique hunter-gatherer than the summer crowd, who browsed and needed an introduction.

I arrived at the shop around eight even though our opening time was usually around ten. Since we were still assessing safety in the new area, now that darkness was more of a constant with the shorter days, I for one wanted to straddle the hours despite the alarm. Thus, for the month, we decided to make early openings on Tuesdays and Thursdays, which tend to bring out the more astute antique browser and collector, then Mondays, Wednesdays and Fridays for the late to rise or career-minded set, who tended to shop later in the evening. We added contemporary "vintage" jewelry for the women who haplessly wandered in for a bauble or two. I know some of our fellow dealers were not in the same mindset as us, but that's us. Those back then were my favorite days: 10 a.m. to 8 p.m. Saturdays were our days when families dragged their children for some reason, and all hands were on deck for the watching of the unattended.

I entered, switched on the lights and disarmed the alarm, which showed a steady light. Thus satisfied, I began my day behind the counter and reached for the ledger, which recorded all the sales, readying myself for a customer. The cleaning people, two women, entered around 10 a.m., as if we were closed. An unusual arrangement, but I didn't argue, as the antiques needed to be carefully handled, and I preferred our presence while they vacuumed and dusted the counters. I did all the dusting of the valuables, particularly the bone china.

All was quiet after they left around early afternoon.

The chime at the front door made its distinctive sound like a wind bell, a purchase I had made while we were shopping in Portugal. I glanced up from my reading of a book Jacques had finished the week before. From my vantage point, I would not see the person entering were it not for the chime at the door.

It was Meg.

She appeared baffled.

"You look uncomfortable. Are you still concerned about yesterday's lights?" I asked.

"I am."

Silence.

"The electricity in this building is old," I observed.

"I will check the fuse box."

"Let Jacques handle that."

The chime went off again, signaling another individual was about to join us.

Meg turned to greet the visitor.

I exited the counter and followed.

There was no one there.

Meg darted to the door, which was already unlocked, a heavy affair made of solid wood, as the building was built when materials used were premium to last. She latched it shut, as it was ajar.

"The wind, perhaps," I offered. A lame excuse considering the weight of the solid door.

Then, as we retired back to the counter, the chime went off again. This time, I emerged to greet the customer or customers and instead met with two men in their late thirties. One had light brown hair, wearing a sharp woolen sweater, and the other, who was shorter, had blond hair and a blue vest. They looked studious and friendly like bachelors at a ladies' party.

"We just wanted to introduce ourselves. I'm Paul, and this is my brother, Jake," said the man with the blond hair and vest.

"I'm Val. I'm one of the owners. My manager is also here..."

Jake waved past me back at Meg, who waved from the back of the store. She'd obviously made his acquaintance. Paul smiled.

"Our cafe is across the street." Paul pointed. "Since we're both new merchants, we thought we'd offer you and your manager a discount. Any lunch item, or breakfast if you wish."

I looked over behind Paul and Jake and noted the press of people still exiting their busy cafe at two p.m. I spotted our two cleaning women carrying coffee on their way out.

"That's very gracious of you two. You can come in and browse our jewelry anytime. For your wives..."

"Thank you. We're also starting dinner for the locals just in case you're open late. Simple things, you know," Paul said.

"How late? We might just..."

"Weekdays until 8, 8 to 8 p.m. Weekends from noon to 5 p.m."

Jake offered: "But Sundays we're closed."

Paul smiled. "Most nights I close up and go home at eleven."

"Whew. Those are long hours," I commented knowing our inventory times and how our hours were straddled.

Jake nodded and handed me a coffee card and a calling card.

"Your husband must have been burning the midnight oil last night," he added.

"Jacques?"

"Tall man wearing a gray suit?"

At this point, I had returned behind the counter where Meg was sitting. I sat on the stool next to her, wondering. Jacques was home early with me – And he never wears a suit to the store.

I was piqued. "Where was this tall man?"

Jake looked back with gravity. "He came out of your store. I was here until eleven."

"What time did he come out? Do you remember?" I made a mental note to ask the landlord if he had stopped by for some reason.

Jake paused. Paul offered, "I left at nine, and Jake saw him too right before I left. I'd say around nine."

I glanced at Meg, who appeared uncomfortable.

"I was going to discuss that with you," added Meg.

"I told her this morning when she came in for some coffee." This was Jake.

I was perturbed and reached for the phone. "Gents, will you describe the man again, please?"

"He seemed tall, slim build, graying hair in a grayish suit and perhaps a tie. He looked very austere."

Jake commented, "I'm sure there's an explanation. He came out the door and turned into the alley there." He pointed to the right of the store.

"You're sure he came out OUR door?" I queried.

"Yes. That door we just entered."

I called Ken, our landlord, and left him a message. Later on, he called back after the two cafe owners had left the store. Ken had not been anywhere near our store and didn't see a need for an after-hours visit either unless we needed him. Besides, he didn't fit the description, from what I can recall. Ken had blond hair and wore jeans like Paul. Plus, the alarm would have gone off, as no one had the combo but the three of us and Ken. He would know to disarm it before entering.

Jacques came over from the old store and later checked the alarm, the bolt and the windows. Then he went to the fuse box. Nothing was amiss. We refrained from calling the police, as there was no evidence of a break-in other than what the two cafe owners thought they saw. Jacques held off sounding a false alarm.

I wanted to meet with Ken and ask why the cleaning people refused to come in at night as they would with most businesses. It wasn't that I wanted them to do so, especially now with the possibility of a breach. There were no cameras at the store, unlike the old one, and I also thought about getting his permission to install some.

"I'll discuss it with him," volunteered Jacques. "But, Val, let this cool down, and let's address it if something else happens."

"You mean wait for someone to break in?"

"No, love. It won't come to that. It's a minor incident, don't you think? Those boys may be mistaken. The alarm works, and the bolt works. Nothing's been tampered with."

Meg watched us talk as she packed her tote for the day, getting ready to leave for the evening. She didn't say a word, but I sensed in her eyes she was intimidated. Finally, she spoke up. "What about the lights? I know I didn't switch them off."

I moved and put my hand on her shoulder. "I'll open tomorrow. You can come in right at ten. Jacques will be here with you until closing."

Not one to be easily frightened, I noted Meg quickly agreed and left. For the first time in our employ, our manager was in a hurry to leave.

CHAPTER 39

"I wasn't one to quibble, but my vision is twenty-twenty. I'm not that old." Paul chuckled with Meg as she recalled. Meg had decided after all to come at eight to open the store with me. She indicated she'd thought about it on her way home the night before while sitting on the train – "what if" scenarios: What if Val encountered the intruder when she opened the store? What if there was a break-in and they were still there at eight when Val opened? Etcetera, etcetera. Dear Meg was protective of her older employer, me. She was so indispensable. I didn't take her for granted.

Meg stopped at the cafe as she had the morning before, right when it opened this time. It was becoming a habit, and the proximity made it convenient. She peered through the glass windows, newly Windexed. Paul was there and so was Jake, busy placing fresh pastries and croissants in the display case, as she recalled, the coffee scent assailing every part of the cafe to welcome the office workers who stood outside waiting.

The door opened promptly, and Meg made her way in, glancing absentmindedly at her mobile and then, in the growing sunlight, decided to turn and snap off a shot of our antique store across the street. Very attractive and vintage, she had said.

It was approximately 8:03 a.m. according to her watch. The darker side of the street was just showing signs of daylight when she snapped her cell phone photo. Unlike where the cafe was situated where the morning's rays had already warmed the countertops, the antique store was still in darkness. Paul gave Meg a broad smile of recognition as she entered with the line of office workers on their way to work. Behind her, two men chatted casually, then were joined by a third. From the conversation in progress, she gathered they were overnight workers at an apartment building, one of the renovated high-end rentals. It happened to be the building they were in: the apartments right above them. One wore the uniform of a security guard, a grandfatherly black man who appeared ready for a long day of sleep after his overnight shift; the other was dressed as a maintenance man, who appeared a bit concerned over some activity in the night. The third man who joined them was the custodian on day shift, still crisp in his uniform.

The maintenance man appeared baffled that the security guard, a portly man, didn't see what he saw: "Seriously. YOU didn't see anything?!"

The security guard jovially replied in the negative: "I tell you, I looked and looked at what building you were talking about. It was quiet."

"Did you even go and cross the street like I told you to?"

"You know I'm not supposed to leave my building."

The man was insistent. "I know you can't. But I wanted to see if there was anyone in the store. There could have been vandals breaking in."

"They were probably having a party above the store."

"That's an office. They store shit up there."

"Well, maybe you thought you saw something when it was a reflection of a party right above us."

It turned out the maintenance man saw "people" coming and going down the store's alley, and music was heard from our store's building.

"I can tell lights and music, Jeff."

"I didn't say you couldn't. It's just that no one lives across the street. Our building HAS parties. That one doesn't." He pointed to the floors above the cafe.

The custodian chuckled. "I hope all's quiet today."

The maintenance man commented: "Yeah, you don't have to worry about that... You're on the day shift!"

Meg finally turned to the group behind her as Jake stood waiting on the customer in front of Meg. "I don't mean to eavesdrop, but I work at the antique shop across the street." She pointed.

The men paused in conversation, observing her.

"Okay, lady, tell us there was some party last night," the custodian queried. Jeff stood waiting eagerly for validation.

"We closed at the normal time. Six."

Jeff's jaw dropped. "NO ONE lives upstairs in that building?"

"No one. Like he said, that's the office and storage area," Meg offered, now concerned once again.

The security guard prodded the day custodian. "He's got some drink." He laughed.

"Can you tell me what you saw exactly?" Meg ventured.

"All I saw was light coming from the back of that store of yours... Like it was in the back alley, you know. Something on fire? Then there's lights flickering."

"Tell her about the music." The guard prodded Jeff, eager to repeat what he had already heard.

"Um, it was, like, not a party kind of music. You know. Not rock or disco or..."

"More like classic music?" the guard offered.

"Yeah. That's it. Classical."

"So it wasn't a party?" the custodian clarified.

Jeff mused, "No, not like that kind of party. It scared the creeps outta me. Never heard anything like it."

Jeff grabbed a pastry as Meg picked up her coffee. He turned to pay as Meg got her change.

"I don't drink. Not even beer." He was serious.

The custodian looked straight in the eye at Meg. "Check it out, lady. If he's sober, there must be something going on up there!"

Meg glanced at Jake behind the counter, who gave her a knowing nod.

Meg opened the door, undid the alarm and promptly switched on the lights. No scents, just silence. As she stood in the foyer, removing her jacket, her mobile dinged, and she checked for messages. Absentmindedly she looked at the snapshot on her iPhone that she had taken of the store from the cafe.

A shadow of what appeared to be a man looked back at her through the glass of the store door. He wasn't smiling and appeared angry.

Meg gasped.

Inches from where she stood was where the man in the photo had been standing, looking out. Then she smelled what seemed like candles or what seemed like several matches being lit. Then the foul scent of burning flesh.

She whirled, expecting something behind her.

Of course there was nothing but the eerie dimness of early morning. The objets d'art stood like waiting soldiers at attention, seeking a home.

Meg ambled to the light switch, casting a glow over the entire vicinity of the foyer and where jewelry lay under the display cases. Quickly, she flicked on each light switch as she went from room to room, dispelling the gloom and silence.

Then she approached the radio and turned it on. The morning news blasted loudly, making her jump.

Meg sat, fumbling with the volume, and sipped her coffee. She realized she still had her coat on, and her handbag still hung from her arm. She took the previous day's newspaper and began fanning the area around her in an effort to diminish the foul smell.

Unable to wait for me, she reached for the phone and called.

CHAPTER 40

J acques took the lead, walking a few paces ahead with Charley the vendor. Charley followed, pulling a large wrapped affair on a dolly. Unloading it with care, the two gentlemen unwrapped it to reveal a beautiful vintage full-length dressing mirror from a German estate sale. It was in perfect condition. Slowly they carried it over to the back furniture room and placed it upright next to the vases and trunk from the Spanish galleon. This was the area furthest from the rest of the rooms, which had a window overlooking the adjacent building and a narrow alley. Jacques reassured Charley that the windows were all secure, the door bolted nightly and the alarm on. However, Charley, ever meticulous, still appeared concerned and wanted to see for himself what the alley behind the building might contain.

The alley had some empty boxes, the detritus of recycled materials strewn about, and an adjoining parking lot of a warehouse. When we arrived there, Jacques inspected the alley for any signs of partygoers leaving trash and the remains of a fire. There were none. Then he approached the store's back window, which looked out into the alley where the chest and the mirror were located right inside. The window was shut and couldn't be opened unless someone broke it. The alarm would go off if all were in order.

He darted with Charley to the parking lot, where there was a guardhouse of sorts, as it was a pay and park arrangement. The parking attendant wasn't there. Then the warehouse, where all the windows were dark, and it appeared abandoned, as warehouses often do. On both sides, I glanced at the buildings and surmised they were various establishments: one was an apparel store and the other appeared a spare parts store. Walking to the next street showed their respective hours ended at five and six, so no one would likely be there to witness anything, let alone have a party. No one would be there as late as 9 p.m. with a party or music.

Jacques scratched his head. "Unless there were teenagers in the alley behind our store, drinking and carrying on, I don't see anyone being here..."

"It must be kids," I surmised.

Jacques gazed back, stupefied. "Playing classical music?"

"Unlikely," added Charley.

"There's nothing there but warehouses and stores, Meg," I offered when we returned.

"I wondered about that," Meg added.

"It's the apartments above the cafe," Jacques surmised.

Charley was in a hurry to leave and sauntered out, satisfied. Meg thanked him, and we heard the front door chimes announce his leaving.

"I need to go. I'll see you at lunch." Jacques made ready to leave, grabbing his keys. A few customers, a lunch bunch, entered and milled about. I smiled and greeted them as Jacques made his way out.

Meg approached me as soon as Jacques left. "You believe the men's story?"

"I do. But I think that they might have heard it from the apartment they were working in, not across the street."

"What about the lights in the back of the store?"

"No idea. Nothing was amiss back there. No trash from a party, from what we can tell."

"The music…"

"From the apartment above them."

Then, her iPhone in her hand, she showed me the photo she had taken from the cafe. Then she told me about the foul smell.

I surveyed the customers around us, contemplating and admiring the antiques. I turned to Meg. "Watch them, please."

I left the store, crossed to the cafe, entered, got a cappuccino from a young girl behind the counter and waved to Jake, who emerged. We chatted about some niceties, and then I left. I didn't want to rehash the morning's conversation, as it was Paul who overheard it.

I looked out the cafe's windows and observed our store across the street. I focused on the door, unconsciously sniffing the air inside the cafe for any foul scents from their cooking. None. I smelled the usual scents of morning coffee, the sweet scent of baked rolls and the bacon. Having taken in enough without undue attention, I left. Emerging out onto the sidewalk, I crossed the street and turned, my back to our antique shop. I stood to observe the cafe and the windows of the apartments above it.

I was hoping to see a poster of the man in Meg's cell phone on a wall of the cafe reflected onto our front door. There was no such thing. What did Paul and Jake see? Did it match the photograph Meg took? If so, who was it?

Five fifteen: I grabbed my coat and checked the alarm one last time, the red light showing it was off, as it should be. I eyed Meg, who appeared tense, and signaled for her to take over the register. Several customers were milling about, some still dressed in work clothes, some obviously retired.

I left for the evening. Wednesday was a late-day closing at the store, where the hours ran from ten to eight in the evening. We had about three hours to go, but the tension made me exhausted.

Later at home our landline rang as we were ending dinner. It was Paul from the cafe.

"Val?"

"Is this Paul?"

"Yes. Meg is here at the cafe."

"Oh. Is she all right?"

I heard an exchange, and Meg came on. "Val, I closed just a few minutes ago."

"Oh? It's seven."

"May I come over if it's not too much trouble?"

I glanced over at Jacques. "Sure. Everything okay?"

"I closed the shop and armed it. I should be there in fifteen..."

"We'll be here."

CHAPTER 41

After I left, Meg spent the better part of an hour helping answer some questions from customers. A few purchases were made, and she was alone again by half-past six when the last customer left. Meg dusted and placed some pieces where there were some new spaces where some artwork and porcelain had been bought.

She then heard music coming from somewhere and found it soothing.

Meg went back to the counter, sat on the stool and began checking receipts against the register.

The music was unusual, she remarked, and seemed like a harpsichord or something similar.

Then the music stopped, and there was a crash.

Meg shot up from her seat. It came from the back room. The furniture room. She emerged and bolted for the back room. Her steps creaked the aged floorboards as her heart pounded, concerned something had broken. Perhaps one of the customers had picked up a piece of porcelain and set it on the edge of a table, where it fell. But in retrospect, she had dusted and found everything in its place after the last customer left. If anything crashed, it wasn't in the porcelain room. She checked anyway. Meg walked into the china area, where all the Lladro and other figurines were kept. Inspecting them, she saw nothing amiss. She paused at the shelves of china, the Imari plates and cups and saucers... nothing. She looked at the British china and noted all was as she had left it just a few minutes ago after the customers had left.

Finally, with reluctance, she slowly made her way to the back room: She entered the furniture room and stopped. Ahead of her, the chest stood at the window, which had darkened with the twilight. Next to one of the vases, the full-length mirror that Charley had placed and secured with a rope to better anchor it sat where he had left it.

But the mirror had a million webs of glass.

It was broken.

Meg saw her reflection broken into a myriad of pieces. She looked behind her and up at the ceiling, but there was nothing that could have fallen onto the glass.

Then she smelled the unmistakable scent of burning matches and then the foul stench of burning flesh.

She touched the glass and saw that the pieces of the mirror were also scattered on the wooden floor.

She picked up one shard, then another, collecting them and placing them on the windowsill.

And that's when she saw it.

She gasped.

A man in profile, in shadow, outside. He stood to the side of the window, close to the glass. Cigarette smoke wafted through the closed window and towards her. It was where the scent of lit matches came from. Cigarette smoke.

In her mind, Meg recollected, hovering just inches from fright, was a feeling of despair and menace.

Glued to the spot, she looked directly at the shadow, which appeared stationary. A sense of foreboding and loss assailed her.

Chills went up her spine, down her back.

The music came on again.

It was in the room.

The music was behind her.

She turned.

No Victrola, no radio. It was in the room somewhere.

Then she turned back towards the window.

The stench came back with force, almost making her vertiginous. Time seemed to pause.

Then the shadow slowly vanished right before her eyes... into the night.

Meg heard a keening sound.

It was coming from her own throat.

Meg bolted from the room.

CHAPTER 42

Jacques placed the phone back on its cradle, thinking. He rejoined us at the little breakfast table off the kitchen, sitting next to Meg and studying her as she sipped her tea. Outside, the dark backyard lay in wait for spring to thaw the cold air, but the chill was within us. Meg was still shivering from her retelling. I could tell she didn't want to think about returning alone the next day. I poured more tea for myself and sat quietly, a pregnant pause in the air.

"The police are going to send a patrol car starting tomorrow evening to check out the alley. They have someone assigned to stop and check the area at night," he offered.

"I'm telling you. I don't think it's a burglar," said Meg.

Jacques studied Meg. "You're thinking the place is haunted."

"Yes."

"Anything could have broken that glass."

I leaned forward. "Jacques, think for a minute. She's…"

"The mirror probably had a fracture that we didn't see."

"Charley would have seen it. I surely would have seen it too," I said.

Meg looked away.

I felt bad for Meg. "I have to agree with Meg. Too many incidents that don't sum up. Who was that man Meg saw in the photo, and who was the one outside the window? The cafe owners saw him too."

"Meg, do you think it's the same man in your picture?" Jacques was trying to piece things together to see who or how many burglars.

Meg pulled out her cell and looked. She showed the picture to Jacques.

I looked over my husband's shoulder. "Is it?"

"I don't know."

"How do you not know?!" He turned to Meg.

I glanced at Jacques, who had raised his voice.

"The one in the window was a shadow."

"A shadow?"

"Yes."

"So what does THAT mean?"

"I can't see if it's the same man. He was sort of in profile."

"Was he the same build, height, hair, what?!"

"I don't know. I wish I could."

"He's casing our store, is that what you think?" I ventured.

Jacques shook his head in frustration. "I don't know."

"Hon, why don't we ask the cafe gentlemen? They saw a man in a gray suit, remember?" I had to offer this to palliate the two. The tension was palpable. It was getting to Jacques.

"Yeah. Let's. Let's go now and ask," he said.

I checked my watch. "It's close to ten."

"I can call first," Meg offered.

"How are we going to explain this to Charley!" Jacques announced to the room, frustrated.

CHAPTER 43

Moisture made the pavement glimmer and lent an aura that made the building more sinister. We parked right in front, as we were perhaps the only two people on the street. I glanced over at the café, and the dark windows stared back at me like an intruder. There were no signs of anyone in the apartments above the cafe. If there were, they were most likely retired for the night or somewhere preparing for bed. We would just have to sit tight until the next day to determine what Jake and Paul had seen, and perhaps if it was the same man, identify him.

But why and how could anyone break in with a bolt and an alarm, break a mirror and not take anything? It didn't make sense, and the more I pondered it, the more I felt Meg had seen a ghost. Jacques, forever a pragmatist and not one who believed in ghosts, needed proof. I hoped we could cross to the apartment building above the cafe to see if we could talk to Jeff, the maintenance man on the night shift.

After the alarm was disarmed, Jacques entered and quickly turned on the lights and made directly for the back room. I followed, wishing we had more people with us. The store felt like a tomb, the cold setting in, as the thermostat was turned down.

The debris, save for a few shards, was where Meg had left it. I walked in and immediately smelled lavender in the impossibly dark and drafty room. The scent was pronounced and cloying. Then the music came softly, but unmistakable.

"You hear that?" I asked.

"Hear what?"

"Listen."

Jacques paused as he reached for a dustpan in a back closet. "I don't hear anything. But I do smell something burning."

Jacques proceeded to sweep the jagged edges and debris from the broken mirror. Only the frame was salvageable of the antique eighteenth-century dressing mirror.

"I can't believe you can't hear that."

Jacques reached for a black trash bag and poured the shards of glass from the dustpan. "Look for something burning. I can smell THAT."

I surveyed the room, then out to the adjacent room where the vases, pots and items such as the blanc de chine statues stood. I proceeded next to the porcelain and fine china area. It was so quiet back there at that end. The music or the scent wasn't present in that room even though there was no door to separate it from the furniture room where the overpowering smell issued from. As if some invisible door drowned out the melody and the odor of matches. I looked up at the surrounding cabinets: there were statues of saints made from alabaster and porcelain. I felt comforted by them as they glanced back at me in serenity. Then I knew, felt, in my heart what might have deterred the scent and the music from entering that room. Perhaps, I thought. Just perhaps.

I returned to the furniture room, where Jacques had just

finished clearing the debris and had tied the black trash bag shut. He glanced back at me as I entered, puzzled.

"I hear it now. Harpsichord music? It's coming from somewhere in this room."

I knew we had no radio, Victrola or any sort of musical instrument. No candles, no matches, nothing lit anywhere, I reported. I smelled my clothing. I wasn't wearing any perfume.

Then I saw Jacques looking out the window. "Jacques?"

He was unmoving, transfixed.

He lifted one finger and placed it over his lips.

I approached the window, stood next to him and looked out onto the alley.

"Do you see it?" he whispered.

I strained to see, but only saw a brick wall, which stood a few yards away.

"To the right by the parking lot."

I turned my head.

"Right there on the pavement."

I focused my eyes. Then I saw.

Jacques looked at me, as I must have gasped. He looked back, and it was still there.

A man in shadow standing unmoving. Whoever it was appeared to be smoking. Or was that smoke?

The sole streetlight didn't seem to penetrate it. It remained undefined, gray and a shadow without a face.

Then it appeared to effervesce into smoke.

Jacques grabbed my arm as we observed it slowly vanish.

Silence.

Jacques appeared rooted to the ground.

Then, tentatively, he reached up... and banged at the windowpane as if to rouse the apparition that had vanished.

A deep silence penetrated our consciousness.

Then a light issued from our left.

I jumped.

A uniformed cop was shining the beam of the flashlight through the alley and approaching towards the window.

Jacques exhaled, and I relaxed.

We nodded as the police officer shined his flashlight towards us in surprise.

I had been holding my breath.

CHAPTER 44

Jacques waved to the cop to wait. He dashed out of the room, and I followed.

Outside, the policeman shut off his flashlight and tipped his hat in greeting. "Good evening, sir, ma'am."

"Did you see that?" Jacques sounded piqued.

The cop paused and shook his head. "See what, sir?"

"There was a man..." Jacques stopped.

"Dear..." I touched him on the shoulder. The policeman obviously didn't see anyone and probably wouldn't believe us.

"I didn't see anyone back there, but I can check." The cop walked down the alley towards the back of the building. We followed.

Of course, the alley and the parking lot were completely deserted.

Jacques turned to me, nodded and thanked the police officer, who continued on foot towards the warehouse.

"Let's go home."

In the SUV, Jacques drove and then stopped at a gas station. When he restarted the vehicle, he had a look that bordered on fright. Very rare for my husband.

"Let's see how things go. I don't want to alarm Meg, so please don't tell her we saw what she had seen."

"But, Jacques."

"Please. Let's discuss a plan."

CHAPTER 45

Meg rang and told us she was ill. A migraine, she said. For now, it spared us having to lie about what we'd experienced the night before. I instantly understood my loyal manager of twenty-four years. She practically grew up in the office and had never taken a sick day until today.

As soon as we entered the shop that morning, we walked to the cafe together and checked with Paul and Jake what they had seen. Other than the man by the front door, nothing else so far. We held off telling them what had happened the night before. None of us had any history on the building or that particular store, and we needed someone who had lived there for a long time. Jake and Paul were also new to the area, having moved from neighboring New Hampshire, where they had been students. Paul retold us what the maintenance man had seen and heard. Meg had shared the photo she took of the front door. I showed the photo to Paul. It was a dead ringer for the man in gray they had seen.

Collectively, the accounts, including what we'd encountered the previous night, told us we were experiencing something otherworldly, it seemed. Logic seeks explanations. Occam's razor always points to facts without assumptions. Meg and I both assumed we were dealing with a haunted store or at least a room – the furniture room in the rear. At this point, even Jacques was veering away from logic to the illogical and bizarre. It was too foreign to us. We needed answers, as we were now on edge.

Jacques called Ken, our landlord, and we agreed to meet about the store and its history. We needed to know what he knew and what else could possibly happen, as we couldn't risk another precious antique being destroyed by what appeared to be a poltergeist of sorts. There were enough signs, but we'd never experienced anything akin to it. I for one didn't want to experience any more strange and frightening occurrences, and I knew Jacques didn't want customers or vendors to begin avoiding our establishment, which we'd nurtured for years. We also were concerned we would lose Meg if the encounters with the strange man continued.

Ken walked into the store, appearing uncomfortable. I approached the front door, locked it, and turned the sign to "closed." It was the first time that I can recall when we'd closed unexpectedly. We assembled behind the counter, and Ken put down a disposable tray from the cafe with coffees, creamers and some scones. I felt he had anticipated some issues and wanted to keep the relationship amicable. We were not the sort to argue, but since we were his new tenants, he would not know.

Ken self-consciously touched his sideburns, which reminded me of Burt Reynolds. He cleared his throat as he offered the coffee. Jacques, not one to pass on sweets and pastries, grabbed a coffee and a scone, intent on making a lunch of them. I sipped.

"There's never been a problem up to now, but there's always a first time, as they say," Ken said diplomatically.

Jacques looked up in the act of adding sugar to his coffee.

"Any incidents of kids in the past in the area partying or playing pranks?"

"Not that I'm aware of. I've lived around here for quite some time. Grew up nearby. Do you remember how this started?"

I went through Meg's first experience with the scents, then the man peering out at the front door, the maintenance man's story, and ended with what Jacques and I had seen. Ken kept nodding, musing and noncommittal. Until I told him about the broken mirror in the back room by the window, which had happened while Meg was alone.

"May I see it?"

Ken surveyed the room, the floorboards, touching the furniture and glancing out the window. He shrugged. "Anything else broken since then?"

I looked over at Jacques. "No. I hope not."

"We had to file for insurance to reimburse Charley. It was in mint condition, you see," Jacques stated.

"I understand. Anything missing?"

I shook my head.

Ken continued to study the room like he had never seen it before. "The police were here?"

"Last night," I qualified.

"They're planning on patrolling on a regular..."

"Yes, I hope so," Jacques said.

Ken looked away.

We waited.

"Ken?" Jacques prodded.

"Before you both made this into a store, it was a warehouse for linens for several years. Before that, a supply store for camping supplies, I think. A bunch of young men and outdoorsy types used to come here."

Ken approached the trunk right under the window. "They

used to have fishing poles leaning against these walls, and there was all kinds of sports equipment. Even boxes of tents."

He nudged the trunk with his foot. Solid. Heavy. "There was one time when a bunch came to get outfitted for some kind of climbing expedition."

"Interesting," said Jacques.

"Then a man, a hobo of sorts, broke in – I think he was trying to steal a tent."

"He loitered around here?" asked Jacques.

"Yes. About ten to twelve years ago when the sports outfitter was here. He was homeless, I guess."

"Was he caught?"

"Yes, but he was released and started hanging out back here... again. In this alley... that parking lot."

"So what did the outfitter do?"

"That's when I installed the alarm. Then the CCTV."

This was news to us.

"There's a CCTV?" Jacques asked.

"There is, but it hasn't been serviced – the circuits outside were damaged and so was the camera."

"Damaged by what?"

Ken pointedly looked at us. "A fire."

I thought of what the maintenance man had said about a glow or a light behind our store.

I warmed to the theme. "When was this fire?"

"Around the time after the hobo stole the tent."

Jacques waited.

Ken continued, "The hobo was apparently hanging out in the alley, was inebriated... as usual..."

"And?"

"What I heard was that he was smoking, and it was dark and cold. He was wrapped in a blanket, as the tent had been returned to the outfitter. The alcohol bottle he had with him accidentally set his blanket on fire. He had lit a jar or fire of some sort to keep himself warm, as some of them do."

I stood, placing my hand on the windowsill for support, looking out in the gloom that was the alley. I tapped the window. "This alley. Outside THIS window."

"Yes. Just a few yards in that parking lot. That windowpane is new, and the bricks outside…"

Jacques stepped in. "You remember how he looked?"

"I never met him, but he was an older man, slim, with a hat. Almost too distinguished to be homeless." Ken looked away. He seemed discomfited, but didn't continue.

"Is he still around, you think?" I prodded.

"No," Ken said. He looked at his watch as if he had another engagement. He drank the rest of the coffee and looked at us both, almost as if he was waiting.

"Perhaps he's still hanging back there in the lot… " I ventured.

"The fire destroyed this wall, this window… he was trying to roll against the wall to extinguish…"

"Oh my…" I gasped.

"Yes," Ken said. "The ambulance came…"

"And he recovered and is now back to his old haunt," Jacques finished.

Ken gazed at me, his blue eyes flecked. "No, Jacques. The ambulance came too late. He died of his burns."

CHAPTER 46

"I need to ask you if you are willing to give me another couple of weeks. The police are now making this area part of their nightly patrol, as you said. Lights back there and in this room might help. If you know what I mean."

Jacques glanced at me. We both knew we had a lease and how it was very difficult to move all the precious items. "We'll stay... unless..."

"Unless?" Ken queried.

I replied this time: "Unless some activity causes another piece of antique to be damaged. They're expensive and can't be replaced."

"I understand."

"We need to be up front with our manager." This I said to Jacques.

Ken strode out of the room and surveyed the rest of the store. Then he turned and came back. He prodded the trunk again with his foot. "Just curious. What's in this trunk, please?"

The chest or trunk was heavy. Solid walnut. It had a bolt of brass.

"I'll get the key," Jacques offered. I walked to the front

counter with him, feeling a sudden drop in the temperature of the room as we left. The knowledge of the violent death just hit home. Ken followed right behind. I sensed he wasn't keen to stay behind in that room either.

Jacques searched in a drawer with Ken by his elbow to look for the key. I went to the back of the counter to tend to a few customers who'd just arrived. I felt a need to compose myself with the daily routine of meeting and selling to customers who knew nothing of the odd occurrences.

A few minutes later, Jacques returned to the trunk with Ken, an ancient key in hand. I followed.

The hasp was open, and the bolt had been carelessly tossed to the floor.

The trunk with its heavy lid was wide open.

I darted over, peering in. Jacques and Ken stood on either side. Inside the large chest were bottles of wine, lying on their sides in a bed of felt. I took out one, and there were more underneath. We began taking them all out, about three dozen in all of what was very expensive wine from Spain. They were collectively over a hundred years old.

Then, as we held the vintage bottles with their contents intact and corked, I smelled the lavender again. That fineness, that softness, that cleanliness. Jacques thought out loud that somehow the man who tragically extinguished his own life by accidentally setting himself on fire must have been sending us a message. I was stunned by this insight from my pragmatic and realist husband. It reminded me of Esteban, my lover of old...

And as we listened to Jacques share his random thoughts out loud, the lavender diminished, and the scent of sulfur, of what we knew now was a burning, took over. Then the stench left me gagging, now realizing what had transpired.

Even in the light of the late afternoon, there was loneliness, a despair I could taste like sour fruit – and a drop in temperature in the room.

That depth of sadness as a memory never left me. I know that Jacques had trouble sleeping that night and the nights to follow. I contemplated leaving and how Meg would react if the haunting and poltergeist activity continued. I thought she was strong enough, but she wasn't. It was too bizarre for Meg, who existed in the land of the living, as we did. A glimpse into the profound sadness of a destitute man, given to drink and hopelessly living on the verge, made us more grateful for what we had. However it left us empty and saddened as if mourning the aftermath of war.

We auctioned the wine as part of a collection we found in that chest from Spain. When it was over, we pulled all the furniture out of the back room, and Ken helped us rearrange the furniture to fit into an area that we had cleared after a series of sales. It took time. Meg would not attend to the store alone, kept to herself and became quiet, almost reticent.

We limited hours unless all three of us were at the store. Meg gave notice at the end of two seasons, brave as she was to stay on for that long, as there was more activity: broken porcelain, unexplained items being moved, and so on. Then she saw HIM again, peering through the back window, gaunt and foreboding, right before the trunk or chest that had contained the wine was finally sold.

The removal of the chest appeared to signal the end of the terrifying sightings of the man, the music that heralded his appearance and the scent of sulfur. However, we had seen enough. Jacques and I retired a few weeks after that sighting and moved out of Vermont and back to Europe. We sold the rest of the antiques by consignment, and a new tenant changed the name of the shop.

That is my story.

PART V

THE BARRISTER'S BOOKCASE

CHAPTER 47
GEORGE

Newport, Rhode Island. The name conjures the grand old mansions, eleven of them a testament to the gilded age of bygone America. The seven that are open to the public, coined the "seven sisters," parallel the seven colleges for women – proud, austere and respected. Their opulence brimmed with forgotten grandeur, standing unsurpassed in building materials and craftsmanship outside of Europe. They symbolized generational success, their facades braving the torrid winds of the tumultuous Atlantic. A punctuation mark at the edge of New England.

The finger of Newport reached down to the Atlantic as if seeking to recline and further luxuriate with eyes to the sea, but that era is gone. Farther inland, the tendrils of Rhode Island, in the form of Providence, sat in gentility with the Rhode Island School of Design within the northern reaches of the city, and on its southwest flank was Brown University, securing Rhode Island as an Ivy League state on the map.

Please call me George. I had an antique shop a brisk ten-minute walk from the campus of Brown. My shop held in its palm the remains of the opulence that we cleared from some of the eleven mansions – which ones, I am not at liberty to tell you, lest I mar the line of respected descendants of such esteemed families. Suffice it to say, we procure these fine and rare heirlooms by default at fairs and estate closings... and some by consignment. For most of us dealers, it was our claim to fame, to hold and sell the unique, rare and artisan objects and furniture that once graced the abode of the highly refined of Newport's history.

In this gem of New England sandwiched between Connecticut and Massachusetts, life swung to and fro in gentle breezes and waves. The susurrus of students adrift among the local populace made for lively evenings as they shared intellectual joie de vivre. Among them, the wings of petrels flap and dip onto and between the rooftops, their rare forage inland hailing cormorants, who mate in their roosts. The cormorants wrestle and fling themselves along the shoreline as they breed, awakening locals and tourists alike before the sound of grinding coffee beans. You can hear the call of the loon and hear the scree of pebbles as birds seek purchase on the loose sand of promontories nearby. When you stand outside my shop, sometimes the salt water stings your eyes.

We were that close to the water.

However, that glimpse of coastal paradise in somnolence by evening was disrupted when we encountered a particular bookcase.

It came in a truck, as most of the larger furniture did. When Eileen and I eyed the furniture that made their way by truck, the unloading was often treacherous, as was the voyage to get to the store. When furniture as well-made, crafted and rare made its way through the streets of Providence, there were often some bumps along the way, mostly from evading traffic and driving on an uneven road. On a busy weekday, it is often a risk we take. Often a scratch or a dent on the oak or mahogany made the piece of art less desirable. This was the case with the barrister's bookcase that came into our possession and was sold in short order to a woman whom we unfortunately got to know, not because of lack of character or conduct, but what occurred since the woman procured the object of desire.

Jean was an art collector and antiques aficionado. She frequented our shop and the shops that mar the landscape of Providence. Her license plate showed she was from out of state in neighboring Connecticut, which for us was not a far drive for the young and vigorous.

I surmised, and so did Eileen, my wife of twenty-one years, that Jean was an acquaintance of my older son Trey, as that was how we got to meet her. Trey was in college at the time in Connecticut and had just moved to a Victorian house in the next town from his university. Soon we discovered Jean was the landlady of the Victorian house Trey was renting with two other undergraduates. Trey frequently drove home from college to help us with the store during weekends, particularly when tourism was at its height, and he conveniently was off from university. It was during one of his visits when he introduced us to Jean, who had already been to the shop a few times on her own several months before, to peruse and enjoy our antiques. Of course, I recognized her, as I have quite a memory for faces.

On this particular visit, Jean was out looking for a barrister's bookcase, which she intimated was a gift she wanted to bestow to her best friend, who was the town librarian near where Trey lived. As Jean surveyed our collection of furniture, Trey shared with me that she had already visited several antique stores in Connecticut, looking for this type of bookcase to no avail. Knowing our incoming inventory that week, our son encouraged Jean to stop by our store for a visit before dining with a friend later in the evening.

For anyone who might not be familiar with a barrister's

bookcase, this bookcase is different from other bookcases in the presence of a glass pane, which usually flips shut over a shelf. Each shelf has its own glass cover, which opens by pulling up and revealing the books. It's quite unique but also utilitarian, as books are kept from dust when the bookcase is made well. Books were a sign of education, and every volume was considered valuable in the days of the seventeenth and eighteenth centuries and thus should be kept protected. They are not as common and are usually made with fine craftsmanship and strong wood. To own books back in the days of the mansions was a sign not just of education but refinement.

On our showroom floor, we happened to have four barrister's bookcases, one of which had ended up with a dent while in transport, as I previously mentioned was a risk. That particular bookcase was made of walnut, a hard and expensive wood. It was made in the eighteenth century, and I recall it came from one of the mansions in Newport, which was owned and passed down privately. Despite the dent on the edge of the bookcase, we were relieved the glass panes remained intact and unscratched.

After a friendly introduction by our son, Eileen took Jean around the store, pointing out the art as well as the antiques. They chatted for a bit, and Eileen left her customer to browse at leisure. Eileen learned our customer was a collector of old books, Renaissance art and figurines. Jean had only begun to browse the furniture when she returned to our area to ask about a particular bookcase. It happened to be the dented one made of walnut.

"I've looked all over Connecticut in the past few weeks," Jean indicated. "And I never found one I liked. Until this."

"Let's look at it and open the shelves, shall we," I offered.

"That would be wonderful."

I allowed Jean to inspect the coveted piece in question after opening the shelves. She seemed very interested and ran her slim fingers across the smooth surface.

"It's walnut, isn't it?"

I agreed.

I strode to the side of the bookcase and showed her the dent, which I had previously polished to remove the scratch as best I could. Where there were flaws, I always made a point to offer a discount no matter how minor, as we honored quality and perfection.

"Oh, that's small."

"Yes, it happened while moving it."

"That's inconsequential." She smiled.

CHAPTER 48

Large purchases were always delivered, as it was our courtesy to the customers, provided they lived less than fifty miles from the store. Darien, Connecticut, happened to be more, as it was farther down the state towards New York. A week passed, then two. Meanwhile, I dusted and polished the bookcase, wiped the glass panes until they shone, preparing it to be viewed one last time by Jean, who paid me in cash.

I thought I would ring her to follow up on when she had made arrangements for the bookcase to be picked up.

"Jean, sorry to bother you, but I just wanted to check on how things were going with the pickup..."

A pause.

"Yes, this must be... (the name of the store)."

"It is. It's George White. It's ready. I can secure the glass and wrap it with movers' cloth when you're ready."

A mumble. Then a cough.

"I'm sorry. Say again?"

"I'm sick. Sorry. I caught a bad cold."

"Oh, I hope you feel better. Should I call at a different time?"

Coughing.

"It's all right. I will call today to make the arrangements," Jean added.

"I will wait for you to confirm the date and time. Get well soon, please."

"I've been sick since you saw me."

"I'm really sorry to hear it."

"Any possibility of Trey bringing it?"

"Trey?"

"Yes. He goes there often, correct?"

"Yes, but you'd need a truck. Our driver only goes less than..."

"Oh, yes. I remember."

"There will be an additional fee should you..."

"I'll pay for it."

I pulled a calculator from the counter and computed, giving her the figure. Mindful she was Trey's landlady, I told her I had subtracted a discount.

"Will Trey drive it over?"

"Hold on, please."

I surveyed the shop and found my wife, who was in the midst of a transaction at the other end of the store. I strode past the register, signaling her of my quick departure out of the store for a minute. I walked to the front door, looked for the driver, who had the truck idling at the curb, getting ready to leave. I waved him over.

A portly man in his thirties, Steve the driver was paid by the hour to transport our rare and precious goods. He was careful and astute about making sure the furniture did not move or get tossed about while in transit.

"Are you willing to drive to Darien?"

"Where is that?"

"Connecticut. Next door." Tongue in cheek. Next door for sure.

He reached for a box and opened a GPS. The first I've seen.

"Hmmm... perhaps. Depends on when. That's over one hundred miles, it looks. Without traffic."

"I know. I will of course pay you extra."

"Hmmm... not sure."

He wasn't going to do it. But I didn't want Trey to take a risk when he'd never driven a truck with an antique in the back before. Knowing Trey, he was a fast driver. Faster than we cared to think about.

"If you will think about it, please," I asked. Eileen and I always took the train into Darien. Besides, the bookcase wouldn't fit in the SUV.

I wrote down Steve's fee, plus tip, and handed it to him. He looked at it, eyes looking about as if we were discussing contraband, and walked out.

"I'll think about it over dinner," Steve added as he unlocked the truck and stepped up into the cab.

I heard the truck's engine turn over, and he pulled away. Then I ran back to the shop and picked up the phone again.

"I'm sorry to keep you on hold, Jean."

"Who were you talking to?"

"I am contracting the driver, but I can't promise transport at this point."

"Not to worry. I just saw Trey go into the house. I will ask him directly."

"No, please. Please. He's..."

She hung up.

CHAPTER 49

I marked it sold with a label and straightened up, the dusk settling in the room as I walked away. I did a cursory inspection of the other antiques and noted the statues from a few months ago had not moved. A cherubim with gold wings stared down at me, eyes of alabaster sightless. It was getting crowded with all sorts of lamps, hat stands, mahogany and inlaid tables, shaker chairs, not to mention the other bookcases and end tables. The walls were heavy with antique framed paintings, prints and wrought-iron filigree parts of sconces and more. I made a mental note to move the inventory around, perhaps to the other room by the entrance, to give them more visibility near the silverware.

I paused to discard a tissue on the floor, probably left by a departing customer.

I heard a cough, then someone cleared their throat.

Behind me.

I turned.

No one was there.

I glanced at my watch and saw a shadow hovering behind me as I looked down. I turned again. It was a trick of the light.

I hastily walked out of the room, flicking the light switches off as I left, casting the room in darkness as I walked. For some reason I felt I was being watched.

As I approached the front room, I heard a hacking cough that made the hairs on my back bristle. I knew there was no one in the room I had just left.

I whirled and made for the switch just inside the adjoining door, but before my hands touched the light switch, I felt flesh brush up against my hand. Perturbed, I still reached for the series of switches, flicking them on one by one. The lights did not come on. I felt flustered, uncomfortable, not one to give in to flights of fancy. I flipped the switches off and on – to no avail.

The darkness remained.

I looked up at the fluorescents.

Then I felt a breath by my cheek, like one exhausted and perhaps dismayed. I yelled Eileen's name, then realized she was outside the store at the curb, packing and bringing in the vintage trinkets, which we placed on a table to attract passersby. That left only me in the store.

I backed away, puzzled. It didn't register in my mind the possibility of a ghost or specter, but rather perhaps an intruder, a prankster.

I began calling out. "Hello. We're closed for the evening."

Silence.

"Hello?"

I flicked the lights on again, and this time the fluorescents flooded the room.

"Please come out, as we're closing. The alarms will be armed."

Silence.

I kept the lights on and darted for the register, making for a bat I kept behind the counter. I grabbed the bat, prepared for what might come.

Silence.

Nothing came.

"Honey?"

I whirled around. It was Eileen, carrying a trayful of baubles and scarves.

"It's nothing. I thought I heard something."

CHAPTER 50

"I can do it, Dad."

"It's not that, son."

"Dad, she's paying me. I need Steve's truck if he's not willing..."

"You're not licensed to drive one."

"Okay, so I'll borrow a pickup. We don't need a truck for that anyway."

I rolled my eyes, worried about Trey driving as he does. A speed demon on the turnpike with a rare antique. It wasn't even the antique that worried me as much as Trey getting into an accident, not used to driving a large vehicle. He had a Beetle.

He touched me on the arm, his brown hair thick like mine at his age. "It's okay, Dad. I won't drive fast. I'm bringing Vicki along."

Vicki. The new love interest from the university prep school. A very nice girl whom he tutored and worked hard to raise her grades. She was hoping to apply to Yale in the spring. I felt better, though I wondered if Jean, who was his landlady, had put the pressure on my son. I questioned it no further, as once Trey made up his mind, there was no changing it.

Several customers were at the store, and I decided that Eileen needed a break. I stood at the register, prepared to assist anyone who was browsing, when I saw my wife walking out of the room where the bookcases sat. That room that left me with a strange vibe. She had a bag of trash in her hands.

"Still dusting?"

"Dusting? Some of these customers don't pick up after themselves!" Eileen indicated, a bit too loud, in my estimation.

I placed my finger on my lip to signal for her to lower her voice and waved one hand about to show there were customers scattered all over the store.

My wife, all five feet two of her with sparkling brown eyes, reacted impishly with a half-grin. "Sorry," she whispered.

I reached for the plastic bag she had in her hand and wondered who was leaving trash in the store.

"They're tissues. Disgusting," she said.

Against my own sense of propriety and hygienic keenness, I opened the bag and peered out of curiosity. "Someone had a nosebleed," I qualified.

She nodded. "Tie it shut and wash your hands. It could be someone who had the flu or something."

I discarded it outside in the curbside trash, which the town had upgraded to some type of attractive receptacle in light of the tourists. Then I paused, thinking, *People with the flu don't usually get nosebleeds. Odd,* I thought.

I dove into the washroom marked "private" and washed to my elbows. I exited the washroom and joined Eileen, who was ready for lunch. We sat opening cans of Pepsi, sandwiches on the counter spread out, wondering what type of tourists were descending on the area.

"Do you think we should disinfect, just in case?"

"I just washed my hands."

"No, I meant the store."

"Where? Near the chinaware?" I jibed.

She chuckled. "No, thank goodness. I found those tissues by the bookcases."

Then it clicked. When I last walked in there, that was where I found tissues on the floor. The lights that wouldn't come on and the hand brushing against me. I told Eileen. We chewed, watched the customers and busied ourselves. My wife was baffled.

CHAPTER 51

Trey jumped into the driver's side of the beige Toyota truck. His housemate Vince had just shut the tailgate to the truck and waved him off, still wearing his pajamas. Riding shotgun was a girl in her late teens with long blonde hair in a ponytail, wearing a Yale sweatshirt and jeans. She appeared shy and wholesome in a way like Shirley Temple. Vicki.

"Don't do anything I wouldn't do with my truck, okay?" Vince jibed, waving goodbye.

"You have my word," Trey reassured him, placing his hands together in prayer.

He looked one last time in his rearview mirror for the pad and the mover's blanket, which Jean had given him to take along just in case the store didn't have any to spare. They sat secure in the truck's bed, pinned by luggage for the weekend stay.

Trey arrived at the store around two p.m. just as a bunch of art students exited our store. We invited the young couple to have a spot of lunch with us before heading to Woonsocket for a weekend at a rental cabin. Trey thought that in light of the distance, he would make a weekend of it, spending time off from studying and the store and returning on Sunday to pick up Jean's bookcase on the way back to Connecticut.

Traffic is usually heavy on a Friday, and what usually took four hours took five. Both looked exhausted despite their youth and welcomed the large lunch we had ordered ahead. Calzones, from what I recall. Trey traipsed in with Vicki, who appeared too shy to hold his hand in front of his parents. She was very sweet.

We sat down and began the customary niceties before unwrapping our lunches, when Eileen broached the subject of the garbage that the "tourists" were leaving behind.

"Just be sure to clean up and wash your hands. There's people coming to the store tossing used tissues..."

"Eileen, please." I put my hand up to stop.

"I know, George. It's not lunch conversation."

"Okay..."

"It's just that we keep the antiques clean..."

"We do."

"... and I don't trust anyone who's touching them with their dirty hands."

"Let's change the subject, Eileen."

"Kids at the store?" Trey offered.

"We don't know, but your father..."

"Eileen, let's not get into..."

"He got spooked."

"Dad?" Trey's interest was piqued.

"I wasn't spooked. You exaggerate," I said defensively to my wife.

"You had a bat in your hand."

"Not a good mix with fine china, Dad." Trey chuckled.

"No shit. I thought there was someone hiding..."

Vicki had turned all shades of pink. It was an argument reserved for a family behind closed doors.

"Hon, do you mind getting some paper napkins in the wash-room, please? I forgot." This was Eileen politely requesting Vicki get some napkins.

Vicki appeared relieved, smiled, and got up from her chair.

CHAPTER 52

Trey watched us from across the tiny cafe table we had gathered at, situated near the registers. As Vicki left for the washroom, two elderly ladies had walked in and were browsing and chatting quietly.

"Do you need any help, ladies?" I ventured.

One in a bouffant hairstyle turned and smiled. "No, please, we're just looking right now. Just admiring the furniture."

I turned back to catch Eileen appearing piqued.

She whispered, "Please don't argue with us when Vicki's here. I don't want her to get the wrong impression."

"I just don't want everyone to know about that incident, Eileen."

"Dad, please tell me. NOW you got me all curious."

"Tell him, George."

Vicki returned and placed a bunch of disposable table napkins on the table near the tomato sauce.

She bit into her calzone and munched, watching us.

"Dad?"

I eyed the napkins Vicki had brought in from the washroom and realized they were the same kind that had been discarded carelessly on our floors. A vision of hobos in New York City's Grand Central Station crossed my mind.

"Well, it was a few days ago when I was getting ready to close the store," I said, inspecting the napkins from the washroom.

"I was outside putting away the fake jewelry..."

"I know, Eileen."

"I'm just saying you were alone..."

"Yes, so I was. We were just about ready to close, and I went to look around for anything out of place... clean up, dust, you get my drift..."

Vicki was nodding, sensing something afoot. Trey's eyes were excited.

"We dust and put away anything out of place, move some inventory to cover empty spots where someone has purchased something," explained Eileen to Vicki.

"Am I telling this story, or are you?" I was getting frustrated.

"You are. Go ahead."

"Go, Dad. I'd like to get to the cabin before dark."

"See, I thought there was a customer still browsing..."

"You missed the good part," Eileen scolded.

"Okay. So I was dusting and picked up some dirty garbage off the floor."

"Tell them where."

"Where you saw the bookcases and ornate lamps or whatever they're called these days..."

"The lamps are Tiffany... they've always been called that..." said Eileen.

Vicki nodded, trying to follow the story, glancing over at Trey. He frowned and looked away, flustered. We were bickering.

"I picked up the trash off the floor, and then as I switched off the lights, there was coughing right behind me."

"And you forgot someone was still in the shop?" Trey asked.

"No one, according to your father," added Eileen.

Vicki was taking it all in. Her eyes were round at this point.

"When I went to switch the lights back on... they wouldn't."

Silence.

"Was that it, Dad?"

"Yes."

"George, you told me..." Eileen shot me a look.

I was done. I wasn't going to mention what might be my imagination. I finished the calzone and stood up, gathering the paper plates. Eileen got the hint and started cleaning up and then walked over to two other customers who had entered the shop.

A hand touched my shoulder. "Mr. White?" It was Vicki.

"Yes, dear?"

"Did you see something?"

Pause.

"No. I felt a hand brush against my hand when I reached for the switch."

"Oh, Dad."

"I know what I felt."

Vicki looked up at Trey.

"That's not like Dad," my son said, within earshot.

"And don't tell anyone else, you hear me?" I knew I was getting testy, but it was a conservative town, and I didn't want any rumors going around.

CHAPTER 53

TREY

I parked the truck at an incline with the cabin to the left. Beyond it was a small pond with willow trees surrounding the perimeter. Very pastoral.

"What was that shop before your parents rented the spot?"

"I don't know."

I was surprised Dad was that sensitive about it. He obviously had a lot on his mind, and the incident that he wasn't anticipating scared him more than he admitted. I brought our luggage into the small living area, glad to be away from school. Vicki had brought some schoolwork, but somehow I knew she was not in the mood, as she had just completed a major project.

At length, we went out to the local seafood place, sat outside to admire the sunset, and the topic came up. Vicki was into the paranormal, having grown up in Old Saybrook, where there were some old and lonely cemeteries nearby that were a rave among local ghost hunters, who were scoffed at and made fun of at the time. Vicki kept her beliefs to herself – until my dad's little incident. I ventured to let her know about what had happened last semester when my friend Lucas and I lived on the beach near the campus.

"YOU sat at a seance?"

"I did. And lived to tell about it."

"What happened?"

"A classmate used a Ouija board."

Vicki looked intrigued.

"Don't get any ideas. I'll never get near one again."

"No, I wouldn't on my grandmother's grave."

"We only did it as there was this wing chair with a spirit in it."

I told her the entire story. The woman in the dorm, the nun who was hurt by some phantom as she was jogging... the way we tried to put it on the edge of the beach to get the tide to take it away.

"Where is it now?"

"Lucas and I trashed it."

Silence.

"I have a feeling," Vicki ventured.

"What kind of feeling?"

"It's not the store... it's something they put in it."

Silence.

"Like what?"

"How long have your parents run this shop?"

"Since I was little... third or second grade, even."

"Did they ever have this kind of weird..."

"No."

"So it must be something new to the store..."

"A new arrival."

"Yes."

"But which one? They get a lot... new consignees, estate sales stuff, new..."

"When did he feel that?"

"The hand? Last week."

"What came in last week? Or the week before?"

CHAPTER 54

That night, I slept fitfully and then finally like a rock. I sensed Vicki get up a few times to get water and then doze beside me. Then I had a dream that Dad was inside the shop and was wandering about, almost like he was lost and stressed. It wasn't like Dad. In the dream, he got sick and was violently coughing. He sounded like Jean, our landlady, when I last talked to her when she'd caught some type of bug. Whatever it was, it was not pleasant. Maybe something was raging, possibly a virus making its rounds on the campuses like it usually does. I felt guilty, as I knew how that got around with students in crowded dorms and cafeterias, not to mention auditoriums, where the general intro classes were held. And we had just been at the store, eating with them.

The sunlight hit me like a drunk at a slumber party, and Vicki was already outside, reading by the edge of the pond. It was warm for an October morning, but I knew the weather was changing fast. I had something deep in my gut besides hunger, left over from the dream or nightmare last night about Dad and his getting sick. The arguing they'd been doing was not like them either. I was hungry from all the driving, but also had a feeling that bordered on dread for some reason. Maybe my parents were starting to get on each other's nerves after being married for so long. I tossed up the nightmare to all the activity we did, like the pressure of Vicki meeting my parents for the first time, though we were not ready for anything real serious yet. Particularly with me still in college and Vicki entering college in the fall, which might be farther than Yale, it might not have been the right time. Maybe it was that and witnessing them bicker about their bizarre story.

I dressed and strode out, walking with a light step, and hoped Vicki was as starved as I was for a big breakfast.

By nine thirtyish, we had collectively tucked into four eggs, ten pieces of bacon and a huge stack of french toast. I told Vicki she ate like a man, and she laughed as she normally did, as she let a lot of things roll off her shoulders. Nothing much bothered her, as she was not inclined to take anything personally. I loved that about her. So bags in hand, we were ready to rock and roll.

I maneuvered Vince's truck in front of the store where Steve usually parked on pickup days. Mom was already waiting, and Dad emerged with another guy I didn't know, carrying what appeared to be the bookcase wrapped in a mover's blanket and secured with ropes. I pulled down the tailgate, and that was when I discovered we had forgotten Vicki's overnight bag.

"Hey, Dad. I gotta go back."

"Forgot something?"

"Yeah. Vick – your bag's not in the cab, is it?"

Vicki stepped off and looked dismayed. "Nope. I need that. Got my term paper and notes for the exam in there."

"Let's load this, and then you can stop on your way home," Dad surmised.

"Just go across Route 44 on your way back... more scenic," Mom offered.

The tailgate up and secure, I looked at the covered hump that was the bookcase lying snugly next to my duffel bag in a bed of blankets.

CHAPTER 55

I coasted onto the dusty pavement of the cabin. Vicki dashed in with keys in hand and was out a few minutes later with her luggage. She stowed it on the floor of the truck's cab, mindful of safety that we might have to stop at some point for a toilet and a snack. She wanted everything within reach without having to exit the cab.

We took 104 down, a slim load, encountered little traffic, and then merged onto Route 116 to catch the large intersection where I would take a left onto 44. The problems began as soon as we turned onto Route 44 and traveled just a few miles down the road, which would take us across to Connecticut. Vince's truck, a Toyota, began to sputter. It was only two years old, from what I recall, and he took care of it like it was his first baby.

I coasted the truck to a stop and noted the mile marker as other vehicles sped by. It was still early in the afternoon, but I wanted to make sure we got help if we needed it. Not that handy with engines, I popped the hood nevertheless, hoping to spot nothing amiss, or if there was, something obvious enough that I could handle it. I inspected the engine and noted the vehicle's newness, gauging from the cleanliness of the carburetor. A bit of dust here and there, but nothing major that you would find when an engine has seen a lot of miles. I touched the hoses, making sure nothing was loose, which I had seen Dad do. I pulled the dipstick, checked the oil, and looked around, searching for the water level. All seemed in order. I decided if it didn't turn when I tried, I'd walk to the closest diner for a pay phone. I looked up, and there was a Cumberland Farms marquee up ahead.

"What happened?" Vicki asked.

"It's okay, I think."

I turned the ignition, and the engine seemed smooth. I re-entered the road and drove.

Cumberland Farms had a few cars parked. Then, a small diner with bright neons in the daytime. I kept driving.

"I was hoping we'd stop soon," ventured Vicki, clearing her throat.

"You hungry?"

"No, I need some water."

Vicki started coughing.

"Just wait a sec..."

I reached behind me where my pack was and realized it was on the flatbed, snug with the bookcase.

Vicki coughed a dry cough. She brought out a napkin from the store and began blowing her nose.

"You feeling okay?"

"Ummm... no. I think I might have caught a cold..."

I flicked on the turn signal, seeing a small farm stand and a barn of sorts. I had just seen signs to Putnam, a small town on the Connecticut border.

Vicki stepped out as soon as I put the truck in park by the barn, hacking. She wheezed, turning red.

"Get some tissues too."

"Got allergies?"

She shook her head.

I dashed off to the barn, a guy opening the door ahead of me. Vegetables, fruits, the fresh scent of plants and hay. I surveyed the area and finally approached an older woman wearing an apron.

"Water?" I asked. She pointed to a glass-front refrigerator adjacent to a rotating shelf with snacks and tissues. I grabbed two bottles of water, some tissues and handed the woman some cash.

"It's two seventy-five."

"That's fine." I handed her more bills, not bothering to count how much I had given her.

When I got outside, Vicki was kneeling on the ground, hacking. It seemed she was trying to expel something from her throat.

"Drink it slowly." I sat down near her, holding the bottle. She grabbed it, drank and then vomited. I touched her forehead, and she seemed feverish.

"Let's get back in the truck."

I helped her in and pressed the tissues in the palm of her hand. I was back on 44 in record time, hoping she could hold on until she could get some medicine and maybe some hot soup.

I floored the truck, trying to make it to Darien by late afternoon. Miles went by.

I observed the trees changing, the leaves now more on the ground than a few weeks ago. The sky was a deeper blue as I sped by.

I must have been daydreaming as I drove, then realized Vicki had been very quiet. When I looked over, she appeared to be shivering.

Silence. I look at my rearview, trying to think. I had the heat on according to the dashboard.

"I'm cold."

I pulled the truck over on the shoulder and realized we'd just crossed 395, a major turnpike, which meant we were already in Connecticut. I pulled a blanket off the flatbed of the truck. I was trying to think what Vicki had eaten and whether eating at my parents' store was a good idea after their discussion of sick tourists. By this time, it was past four, and I was beginning to think of stopping to rest.

"I know you're not feeling well. Do you think stopping to have soup and something to eat might help?" I was thinking of the grill up ahead. She shook her head. I touched her forehead, and she was definitely burning up. I turned the motor and slid back onto the macadam.

"You think you can drink more?"

"No."

I kept driving.

Crap. We passed the grill. I had to pee.

I just had to think about what she ate and what was making her sick. Whatever it was, she was more susceptible than me.

I coasted onto a broad shoulder when I spotted a wooden shack marked "Toilet." A rest stop. I spotted a sign: we were now driving through part of Natchaug State Forest.

I touched Vicki, who appeared to be slumbering under the blanket. She was still shivering even with a coat on. I walked to the edge of the tarmac, looked back at the truck, deliberating. I rushed towards the toilet and realized I hadn't locked the truck. I turned back and opened the door.

Vicki was hacking away.

"I'll be right back, okay? Lock the doors."

She nodded, eyes bleary.

I slammed the door and bolted for the men's room.

CHAPTER 56

I came out to find Vicki standing outside, wrapped in the blanket, staring at the flatbed of the truck. Her cough had subsided, but she had a Kleenex pressed to her mouth as she eyed the flatbed.

"Ready? What's up?"

She turned to me and pointed at the bookcase, Kleenex pressed to her mouth.

The bookcase, which I had laid flat with the glass door up and covered in blankets, was uncovered. The ropes, which had secured it to the blankets, somehow were loose and untied. I approached the bed. Someone had definitely untied the ropes, and the glass panes were exposed. I turned to Vicki. "Did you..."

She began coughing in the act of trying to talk. "Why would I?"

"Who was out here while I was in the toilet?"

"I don't know."

"Does that mean there WAS someone?"

"No. I don't think so."

"Why did you come out of the truck?"

"I had to get some air… can't you see I'm sick? I'm trying to stretch…"

"You said you were cold!"

She darted a hostile look my way and began coughing and sputtering. "YOU came out and got the blanket covering it." She indicated.

"No, that's a different one."

"Well, I didn't touch your antique."

"I'm sorry."

She paused to take a breath. "Is that all you care about? That damn bookcase?"

"What? Don't be like this."

I approached her, but she recoiled. I pulled the blanket from the sides of the bookcase and wrapped it over the glass panes as before. A stiff wind blew the trees around us as if bidding us to leave. An ominous cloud threatened rain.

"We need to get inside. Please."

Vicki pulled out another tissue and covered her mouth as she clambered into the truck. I covered her with the blanket, and she stiffened.

"I need to get this to Jean. That's all."

Coughing.

I jumped back into the driver's side and turned the ignition.

Vicki opened her door and jumped out.

"Where are you going?"

Vicki darted towards the restrooms. I clambered out and locked the truck, following.

The trees around us were swaying as if they were about to break. In my mind, I thought, oh no. The bookcase will be soaked by the time Jean gets it.

I watched Vicki run around to the back of the restroom shack.

I turned back to the bookcase. A light flashed. I looked up, and the sky appeared darker.

Lightning.

I scurried, pulled the truck's tailgate down, hoping Vince kept a plastic tarp in the bed. I walked around the truck, searching, looking in, touching the sides for some compartment I had hopefully missed. The storage bin towards the cab. Locked? It opened. Art supplies, brushes and cans. Vince's art supplies. He kept them there for when he drove to the beach to paint. Son of a fortune. Wouldn't he keep a tarp to cover his canvases? Something blue peered back at me from under the bookcase. I clambered up and almost fell onto one of the glass panes in my rush. Reaching down, there it was, still folded neatly.

"Thank you, Vince," I said out loud.

Unfolded and wrapped. Then the wind blew, and the tarp slid off, almost blowing away.

"Shit."

I bolted for the nearby wood.

Rocks. I scurried and grabbed some sizable ones and realized Vicki was still in the restroom.

The tarp was sailing my way, as if after me. I darted after it as the wind turned, almost missing the edge, the bright blue a stark contrast against the darkening forest.

I tripped on the tarp's edge as I ran. The rocks fell onto the ground.

Gathering them, I grasped the tarp as the wind blew again.

I eyed the restroom, willing Vicki to emerge. Where was she?

Back to the truck bed, I climbed, spreading the tarp over the bookcase and securing the heavy rocks to the sides.

Then I made for the restrooms yards away.

CHAPTER 57

"Vicki?" I walked around, found the door marked "Women" and banged on it. "Vicki?"

Silence.

I looked around, then opened the door.

Three stalls and the acrid scent of urine assailed me.

All the steel doors were open.

I emerged, surveying the wood around me. Wind chilled me to the bone, moisture accumulating with it.

"Where are you?"

Wind blew, almost singing.

The cold began to leach through my parka.

"Vicki!"

I spotted her weaving through the wood, approaching, her coat's hoodie over her head, still wrapped in the blanket.

She looked up and darted towards me. I was beyond relieved.

"Why did you..."

"There was a creepy woman in there..."

"What?"

"I'm getting in. I'll tell you when I get back in the truck."

Something clanged open, like a door. I opened my door, checked Vicki's and slammed mine shut.

I drove through the park and then realized I hadn't checked to see if the tailgate was secure after I put the tarp on top of the bookcase. Perhaps that was what clanged open. We were now almost out of the park, and the isolation of the road had a sense of loneliness instead of serenity.

Rain descended, thrumming on the cab's roof.

I parked, exited the truck and ran to the tailgate. It was down, and the bookcase could have slid right off into the road. Strange. I latched and secured it. Tissues littered the back, but I made no comment to Vicki, as she might think I was accusing her of littering too.

We drove the rest of the way to Harford, through a rest stop and down finally towards Fairfield County. Vicki remained quiet the rest of the way. I stopped to get dinner, and she shook her head, sullen and quiet. I drove on. I parked in front of her parents' house, and she quickly grabbed her overnight bag and made her way towards the front door without pausing to say goodbye.

"Are you going to tell me what happened in the restroom?" I yelled as I stepped out to accompany her, hoping to explain our delay to her parents.

She kept walking, reached the door, opened it and shut it.

CHAPTER 58
GEORGE

Jean called the store and exclaimed how the bookcase looked great in her living room. She had polished it, got the glass cleaned, and took a picture with some figurines inside the glass cases. She would wait until her friend Beth's birthday was close before surprising her with it. Meanwhile, she would enjoy looking at it.

We were relieved despite the setbacks Trey had en route to her house. Trey would not discuss the trip back, which Eileen and I gathered was not pleasant. He would not discuss Vicki, and we told him she seemed like a very nice and decent girl. She got sick on the ride back, he said. He too had developed a cough, and as the days progressed, we wondered if his childhood asthma had returned from the way he sounded. Then, a day after he had dropped off Vicki and finally unloaded the bookcase at Jean's house, he was back to his old normal self. He called Vicki to check in on her, hoping she was willing to talk, and she had miraculously recovered as well. No lingering coughs, sniffles or sore throat, let alone a fever. Perhaps they were both exhausted and stressed.

Trey was juggling a heavy workload as a new chemistry major, having switched from art, so Eileen and I worried he was getting run-down. We didn't even know he could do that in his sophomore year at the university, but apparently he could. He also had long hours at our store almost every weekend, which was his idea of learning the business, just in case med school did not become a reality. However we thought he was working too hard, drove too much, so it explained how he quickly got sick. Something was going around the campus, and we almost opted out of a chamber music concert at Brown, but we discovered the flu had not reared its ugly head yet at the campus.

"So what is this going around?" Eileen asked me. I didn't know. A different strain. We met up with two other couple friends who worked for Brown and surmised that somehow the coughs were confined to the shops in our area. Actually, only in our store, they laughed.

We laughed it off until the two elderly ladies who had entered our store while we were having lunch with Trey and Vicki came down with a bug. The woman with a bouffant hairstyle called to tell us something made them sick at our store right after their visit. I felt so bad I offered them both a hefty discount on some Royal Staffordshire china tea and cup sets if they chose to come back. It was all I could do. She asked if some of the antiques were imported from some far-off country where there might have been some form of illness traveling about. I honestly couldn't offer her an answer.

Strangely, as soon as some of the inventory was sold, the coughing and tissues on the floor and tables of the shop disappeared. I just didn't know how to explain it in all our years in the business, but they must have carried some virus or bacteria on them. Jean's bookcase happened to be one of those that were sold that same week. We've never heard of inanimate objects carrying diseases.

Then the worst happened. I got another call from Jean about the bookcase.

CHAPTER 59

Trey watched Jean at her stove, a huge Wolfe with six burners. It was only four p.m., but she was already busy preparing a lavish dinner for a small gathering of friends. She had invited Trey to stay, as he had just run an unexpected errand for her again when he dropped off the month's rent, buying some spices at the local Indian store. She didn't take cooking lightly and spent hours like she did with antiques, searching for recipes on the internet and attempting to copy dishes from restaurants she frequented when in New York City. She didn't have to stray far to find excellent and authentic foods as a foodie. She had a penchant for mixing the right ingredients and made dishes that made dinners with friends a pleasure. Until she got the bookcase.

As Trey's landlady who lived in the next town, Trey and his roommates were kind to her, as she lived alone. The boys even drove the woman to New York to pick up pastries, as she was frustrated over her little community of neighbors, whom she described as "pedestrian," for their lack of sophistication in baked goods. Jean was not really an elitist in that sense, but was just a picky connoisseur when it came to authentic foodstuffs.

On this particular day, Jean was in her kitchen, preparing another lavish meal for a small group she expected for dinner who loved Indian cuisine. Trey had been watching her use the spices he had just bought for her, and she was showing him how she used them for the lamb roast that was now in the Wolfe's oven.

Then she began to feel unwell, asking Trey for his assistance in chopping up the okra and eggplant for the side dishes. It had only been a few days since Trey had dropped off the antique bookcase when she began to feel dizzy and feverish. At her request, Trey darted up the stairs to her medicine cabinet and watched her push a thermometer into her mouth. She told him she had just gotten over the flu, but now her throat began to get scratchy again. Trey watched signs that were now becoming too familiar. He was hoping she would cancel.

Jean reached over her large well-appointed stove, a study in pale blue, to shut off the gas oven, which housed the curried rack of lamb she had so lavishly prepared. She had stressed over the meal, from what Trey saw, and was indeed on the edge of canceling when her best friend, Beth, the town's librarian, called.

"I got a surprise for you."

"Oh? Tell me."

"Then it won't be a surprise."

"I have to warn you and Dean that I just developed a cough."

"Do you have a fever?"

She looked down at the thermometer. "Not sure, but I think I might not be up for a late evening."

"That's fine. Dean's tired anyway. Did you call the Cunninghams?"

"Not yet. I'm really sorry about this." Jean looked up at Trey, signaling the dinner was off. Trey shrugged his coat on, placing the change from the spices on the counter, glad to go home.

"The roast will keep until you get better," added Beth on the phone.

"I'll take a raincheck on the surprise. I might as well tell you I have one for you too. But it's for your birthday."

Trey didn't mean to eavesdrop on the conversation, but was feeling well again and now felt he might have passed on the flu to his landlady. Vicki had definitely caught something, but he was happy she had recovered in twenty-four hours.

Trey added as he opened the back door of the kitchen, "It's only a twenty-four-hour bug." He winked.

Jean coughed, smiled and nodded as he left.

CHAPTER 60

I t wasn't a twenty-four-hour bug. Jean was not getting better this time from her cold. It was pneumonia. She called from her hospital bed. The doctors prescribed a regimen of medication and confined her for a few days. I breathed a sigh of relief, glad that it was caught in time. But it wasn't over. In the interim while Jean was in the hospital, Beth was house-sitting, as Jean was a single woman who was divorced with no children, and her home had a lot of expensive items, including antiques.

Beth's account clarified for us finally what might be the string of infections that began with the tissues in the store I had found on the floor – while closing that day, a phantom hand touched mine. Beth had herself and her husband tested for TB, as she felt the signs of the sudden flu pointed to something more infectious. They were both negative. Upon arrival at the house, which she later disinfected as a precaution, she noticed a lingering smell of illness, which she could not describe, but had experienced when her own mother was dying.

Hours later, as was customary for Beth, she settled down with books to read from the library and a basket of knitting after doing the cleaning. She'd also brought an antique book, which was the surprise she'd had for Jean before the dinner party had to be canceled. Unbeknownst to her, Jean had purchased the barrister's bookcase, now temporarily in Jean's living room, as a gift for her upcoming fiftieth birthday. After wrapping the antique book and placing a card on it, Beth left it on top of the bookcase and went home to her own house.

Monday she returned after working at the library and decided to make dinner for her husband, Ron, on Jean's stove, which she loved. Again, she disinfected, wondering where the acrid smell of sickness was coming from. By the time she was done, exhausted, she finally cooked as her husband watched, marveling at Jean's high-end kitchen.

At the end of dinner, Beth dialed Jean's room number at the hospital to check in. As they were talking, she mentioned how she loved cooking on her large stove, wiping it spotless as they talked. Ron walked by and waved goodbye as he exited via the kitchen door. Beth distinctly remembered waving back, wondering why he was already leaving.

Satisfied Jean was on the mend, and X-rays revealed she did not have tuberculosis based on a negative tine test the week before, Beth settled into her knitting in the family room. She had just sat down and then heard her name being called. It sounded like Ron, her husband, had returned.

She walked over to the living room. "Oh, you're back."

"Back? I've been here waiting for you."

Puzzled, Beth glanced at the hallway and towards the kitchen. "I saw you wave and go out the kitchen door."

Ron just stared at her, a book in his hand. "I've been here all along, listening to you talk on the phone."

Beth looked at the old book in Ron's hand, bound and ancient. She immediately recognized it.

"I got it from Jean's bookcase. An antique first edition – Dickens," Ron clarified.

The barrister's bookcase was in the living room near where Ron sat on a high-back chair, adjacent to a fireplace. The top flyleaf was open, the shelf, like the other shelves, empty save for a few figurines.

"You unwrapped it!"

"Oops. This book was wrapped?"

"That's my gift to her. Remember?"

"I found it in the bookcase."

"Why did you unwrap it?"

"It wasn't wrapped."

Beth put out her hand, and Ron handed her the book. "I have to wrap it again now."

Then he began coughing, almost turning red.

"Are you okay?"

He didn't stop.

Beth dashed back to the kitchen and returned with a glass of water. Ron drank, handed the empty glass back, and stood.

"Here."

Beth took the glass and happened to glance down at the floor – and recognized the card that she had purchased with the wrapping. Very puzzling.

"If you didn't unwrap my gift, then who did?"

Ron looked around, searching the room. "Don't know."

Beth sighed and stuck the card inside the book.

With that, he walked down the hall and turned at the front door. "I don't think you should stay overnight."

Beth placed the book on the coffee table next to her basket of knitting.

She walked back to the living room, where the bookcase stood, and gingerly shut the glass door, backing away.

She turned back.

"I'm leaving." Ron reached for the doorknob.

"Dear."

"Yes."

"Are you sure you didn't pass me in the kitchen?"

"Why would I lie about that?"

"I could've sworn..."

"Come back with me and bring the book."

"Is something the matter?"

"There." Ron pointed to the bookcase.

"Okay, you're making me uncomfortable."

Ron began coughing again. "Look."

The bookcase's top glass door was open again.

"Let's go," Beth said, bolting towards the door and passing Ron out the door.

"Keys?"

"Oh, sorry." Beth re-entered, grabbed the keys from a plate in the foyer and walked out.

"You left the book," Ron added.

Beth ran back in, exited this time with the antique book and her basket of knitting.

Beth locked the door.

While she turned the bolt, Beth distinctly heard a woman coughing through the door. She turned to Ron with a look.

"No one's there. Go."

They dashed to the street.

CHAPTER 61

Beth told Jean what Ron had experienced in the house and what she thought was Ron passing by her in the kitchen. They both heard the coughing when they locked Jean's door. The next day, the couple returned together and found Jean's handkerchiefs on the floor around the living room near the bookcase. As if someone was sick and neglected to pick up after themselves. This time the top flap to the bookcase was shut.

Jean called me from the hospital, asking about the origin of the bookcase. I had, regrettably, no history on who was the previous owner or the one before that. I made a point of visiting her to explain how we'd acquired it. I went through the process of acquisition, such as who authenticated the bookcase and how we appraised it. There was no doubt it was made in the early 1900s – 1910 to be exact – and the imprint of the maker was unmistakable on the shelves. What troubled her was the line of people who claimed to become sick when the piece of antique was around, including herself.

Eileen and I visited at length with Trey, getting more details of his difficult trip on the way back to Connecticut with Vicki.

Sudden coughing and a fever seemed to be connected to the antique and the bizarre appearance of tissues. So strange were the events that we didn't know whom to call or consult. I called the other new bookcase owners, wondering if the store needed to be disinfected. It was a series of difficult calls, as we didn't want anyone thinking we were harboring some disease at our store. No one else corroborated our experience. The other pieces of furniture were fine and were "tastefully elegant," as some of the new owners put it.

Then Steve, our hired truck driver, explained how the bookcase ended up with a dent, after he overheard our conversations at the store when we were attempting to make good on what we needed to do about the bookcase. His account made us realize that the bookcase needed to be with its original owner, but it wasn't possible, as it came into our hands only because it was for sale from the estate of the deceased.

The deceased.

Steve's story was brief but no less bizarre, if not downright creepy. After securing the bookcase among other antiques in the back of the truck, he emerged from the back and hopped down to the pavement. He was about to light a cigarette with his hired hand to take a brief break. He turned to pull down the panel door when he distinctly heard someone cough inside the truck's container. He turned to peer in, but no one was there, of course.

He pulled the sliding door down and turned to secure it, then lit up. This time they both heard a cough issue inside the container. The younger man laughed nervously. He unlocked the truck, hopped inside and checked, thinking someone was stowing themselves in the container. Strange. They drove through Providence when someone honked at them and told them the back was open.

Steve stepped out, ran to the back of the truck in the center of traffic, and discovered the door was halfway up. Inches from the edge was the bookcase. It had somehow made its way to the back of the truck though it was tied securely to the walls of the truck. One side had hit the door, and that was how the dent was made.

Jean would not return to her house until it was removed from her home. Eventually, Beth volunteered to take it to the library and see if they could store it in the attic of the building. Beth appeared to be the only one who didn't get sick from being near the bookcase. That was when Jean finally disclosed it was a surprise gift for her fiftieth birthday, which was coming up. Graciously, Beth took the bookcase out of Jean's home before her birthday with Trey and Vince's help. The short trip was uneventful, and they carried it up to Beth's attic up in the cedar-shingle home she shared with her husband. Ron didn't want it in the living areas of their home, as it had also "infected" him while he was in Jean's home.

There the barrister's bookcase sits in darkness. Alone.

CONCLUSION

Haunted houses, facilities, cemeteries, people and objects. What do they have in common? In all my years of hearing accounts, compiling stories from all over the New England states and later all over the globe, I noted similarities in these hauntings.

In the case of the wing chair I purchased long ago, the young woman must have died suddenly under tragic circumstances. We pine, we crave and we covet. When we do finally possess whatever it is we desire, we hold on to them - until life somehow is cut short. When that happens, we can't let go - and in some cases, as I believe this case to be, the deceased needed to hold on to her possessions. We see a soul disembodied, holding on and even coming with a vengeance to reclaim what was hers.

For Augustina, the urn was part of a collection, something merely for show in her growing Chinoiserie. However, there was an unfinished life within who passed in violence. The urn came with a guardian - one who made the family aware that the spirit needed closure - and it finally got that. Once the rite was complete, the guardian never appeared again.

For Sam, the lithograph unraveled his weaknesses: his

ethnic identity in crisis came to consciousness, the sense of sudden loss and inexplicable betrayal triggered psychic chaos. It loosened his mind from its moorings. Sam needed validation for what he experienced in the land of the incredible. In the end the validation he craved came in the form of a woman who defied his own rigidity and nature.

For Valentina, the move to a larger store tucked farther away from the familiar was too unfamiliar. It was horrifying. In changing her worldview, she discovered that her husband was more open to a new experience than she believed him to be capable of. By keeping a pandora's box in the back room, which held a coveted set of items, they unwittingly invited a spirit who died painfully and remained addicted even after death.

George and his son Trey never thought they would be transported back to an era where consumption (tuberculosis) took lives of the young and vibrant. In that treasured bookcase was the energy of a young woman who loved books and kept them protected in a barristers bookcase. She wanted them to know how she suffered, touching anyone who dared to take or transport the bookcase - with her illness.

When we pass into the next dimension, we pass with only our spirit. However a sudden and fatal tragedy can stop us from gaining that insight. We know we can only take our memories and relive the lives we lived. To learn and hold dear those we loved and loved us - and to move forward into the everlasting life we so deserve knowing we are who we are and the world beneath us is richer because of us. But for those cut off brutally in youth or in the prime of their lives, hanging on to what they know can be their last hope of living fully.

Thank you for reading this book.

SNEAK PEEK: THE TALISMAN

As a bonus, the following pages contain a few chapters of a book in progress. This true story, which I have made into a nonfiction novel, is pieced together from a longtime college friend. I shared his father's story of the haunted barrister's bookcase, and now his story of what he heard and subsequently discovered about the history of the Victorian house he rented with two other college housemates. He now lives well away from this house and its "tenant."

CHAPTER 1

Chevalie climbed up the tree and surveyed the neighbor's yard below. Just yards away, a dog of indeterminate breed was sniffing the body of a dead animal on the ground. It was lying right outside the kitchen window of the Scott widow next door. The dog whimpered as if beset with ennui, a sadness Chevalie felt with a tartness that tasted of green apples from the local produce store. From her vantage point that early Saturday morning in the vast neighborhood outside Edgewood Park, she sensed a oneness with the dog. The loneliness of the sole animal as it surveyed the vast hollow of loss tinted the external landscape with a blueness that mirrored her own blueness within.

Chevalie peered for a closer look, then inched her way towards a higher limb, her small athletic frame limber from her gymnastic days in fourth grade before she stopped when she entered middle school. Her approaching teen figure made her look gawky, according to her mother. Her distressed jeans caught a tree limb, distressed way before fashion dictated it was fashionable. They were just simply old and dotted with holes, as she only had two pairs, one in the wash.

Furiously, she pulled at the twig that snagged the pants leg. Then it cracked, giving way to fall soundlessly below.

The dog looked up at the sound.

Her tee shirt, once white, was now a study in leaves and detritus from her efforts to climb and see. She was born curious and avid for the strangest of adventures, but she knew she would need to toss the outfit in the wash before her mother saw her. Her dark brown hair almost covered her deep large eyes, which widened with surprise when they fell across her face.

It was a dead cat.

The dog made eye contact with Chevalie. His sorrow was as impenetrable as hers, as she realized in that awful moment the inconsequential death in an inconsequential neighborhood of an animal that had passed alone in a yard replete with the remains of an untended garden. A thick bump formed in her throat, and she willed herself to swallow what she was seeing as the dog left the carcass untouched, heading to the owner's back-yard for a drink of water.

She followed the dog with her eyes and decided that, unlike her, the dog was, perhaps, loved. She surmised he was young, as she had not seen him last year when she entered eighth grade. Or perhaps she did not notice him, as she was so deeply absorbed in a book that consumed her being and stretched her "knowing-ness" to things that were before out of reach. The public school didn't teach what the book did.

The dog lapped at a bright blue bowl sitting next to a matching toy panda. Pandas in blue were a rarity, but this one appeared special. It appeared cleaner from a distance than her shirt and jeans close up. Her mother was a neat freak and vented at the slightest evidence of dirt. She could tell cleanliness a mile away, it seemed. It tinged her with anxiety every time she re-entered the house, knowing of the woman's disapproval and resultant betrayal of people and things below perfection: a manifestation of her own inadequacy mirrored in her daughter's inability to stay clean. Thus, Chevalie didn't trust herself to be clean enough, to be good enough. Her belief in herself was inexorably intertwined with her mother's innate disapproval; Chevalie, a version of her mother's incomplete self.

The penumbra of incompleteness pushed Chevalie out of the tree and onto waiting ground. It was time to wash and try to remain clean again and, perhaps, be loved. Then she overheard a door past the wooden fence slam open, and the dog yelped. Chevalie darted to her side of the fence and peered through the slats. A woman in a thick coat and polyester pants had emerged and struck the dog with a folded newspaper. Not painful, Chevalie surmised, but an insult to the dog, which was trying hard to please its owner. Chevalie gritted her teeth at the injustice, as the woman with curly dark hair in her fifties, plump and overfed no doubt, pulled the dog by the collar inside. Minutes later, the woman re-emerged with a black plastic trash bag. Chevalie followed with her eyes and pushed at the old fence to part the slats to allow her a view. The woman picked up the dead cat and tossed it unceremoniously into the bag.

A zip tie followed – and a life was done.

An ode to a pet dead before old age and a dog reprimanded by virtue of his proximity. No burial, no words, no tears. Just a plain plastic bag and a zip tie.

Chevalie darted away, anger welling in her. It was time.

CHAPTER 2

Into the room with grapes on a trellis – her wallpapered room, up on the third and highest floor. Chevalie's wooden bed stood by the window, littered with signs of a girl turning towards books and a plain curiosity for things beyond the view of her window: a volume with a plain black cover, another showing a manga-style cover of a boy with dark hair, a music box overfilled with costume jewelry – but in plain sight a drawing of a hex sign, perhaps.

Around the room there was femininity: lace light blue curtains to allow the sun and magnify an otherwise uncertain sky, a dresser hand-me-down with combs and all sorts of dime-store candy, a walk-in closet and a bookcase filled with Nancy Drew. Across the bed near the door was a desk, small and pock-marked, but it appeared to be sturdy and almost oak. There sit open books from school, nondescript and exhausted. Then a larger, dark-covered one, obscured from full view by textbooks. It was a hardbound book, the spine tinged in red. Almost fore-boding in size and thickness.

Chevalie entered, cleared her bed and stacked the stuff from the bed on the dresser nearby. She sat on the bed, pulled down the shades and undressed, tossing the clothing into a hamper inside an open closet. She leaped into the shower of a club-footed tub, ancient in the adjacent bathroom. She unhooked her bra and studied the fracture breaks in the tile of the old bathroom as she did.

She turned on the showerhead and entered the spray. It soothed her as she allowed it to caress her face and arms. Visibly her anger from watching the woman dissipated with the water. She clicked her tongue against her cheek as she showered.

Click, click.

In school, students turned to Chevalie seated towards the back when she did this clicking sound. It announced boredom, even disdain for the humdrum subject matter.

A boy with ears bell-like, almost Disney, looked back at her from his front seat, hearing her click her tongue to announce to others nearby that something was amiss. He studied the middle-aged teacher in a frayed sweater and pumps, skirt hitched in the back. He gestured with his finger at the teacher's back, addressing the class with gestures. The teacher was scrutinizing someone's homework in front of the room as she leaned sideways by her desk. Mickey Mouse, as he was affectionately called, finally couldn't stand the puzzled looks others gave him in exchange: "Hey, look. She forgot to pull down her dress," he finally whispered.

"Click, click," went Chevalie's tongue again on her cheek; she suppressed a huge smile as she watched the middle-aged teacher lean down to scribble corrections, her skirt hiked up to reveal the edge of her panties.

Laughter, hoots.

The teacher looked up, surveying and scrutinizing the source of the laughter. Her dress, still hiked up from probably a hasty recent trip to the ladies' room, was moving around, making her look like a duck. Haste makes waste.

They laughed, knowing Chevalie, who was well-liked for her noncomforming attitude and panache for dressing cheaply but with a certain style, would not get in trouble. She might even be commended.

"Mrs. Misquamicut."

"Yes, Chevy Lynn?"

Chevalie slid one foot out of her desk, stood up and, like a soldier, came to attention.

Mrs. Misquamicut turned her head sideways, puzzled. "Yes, sweetie?"

Laughter. The teacher darted an angry look at Mickey Mouse, even though most of the students had laughed.

Silence.

"Miss..." Chevalie slapped her own butt, to indicate the teacher's dress in back.

Mrs. Misquamicut darted a look bordering on embarrassment, then touched the back of her dress. "Oops," she said as she tugged at the dress, pulling the edges off the waistband of her panties. She turned bright red for all to see.

The boys looked away, chuckling; the girls appeared shocked, some bored and some smiling at Chevalie conspiratorially.

"Thank you, Chevy Lynn. These boys would have let me go on if it weren't for YOU."

Laughter.

"Silence!" Mrs. Misquamicut reached for the hall phone by the classroom door to summon the vice principal. Chevalie sat back down, placed both her hands in repose on her desk like a dutiful pupil. The students looked sideways, waiting for a blame game to begin. Some looked at the clock. Mickey Mouse stuck his tongue out at Chevalie, and she offered back a middle finger when the teacher began talking on the phone to report the invisible culprit.

To Chevalie's classmates, she was a comfort, knowing their compass was correct, validating their growing antiestablishment bent towards adolescent individuality. In today's lingo, Chevalie "got it." However, she tricked them: deeper inside her was a hollowness foreign to them all. Chevalie harbored a pain indescribably stagnant like the community pond next door, where the koi froze and never recovered from the winter freeze. A foreignness that could not be validated by others in the form of alienation by those she hoped would love her. This they did not share with her in their houndstooth vests and Sunday best as they drank Kool-Aid, Tang and ordered egg creams from Horn and Hardart. She was a part, yet remained apart; thus she remains, inexorably, alone.

The shower shut off, Chevalie stepped out, hugging a thick white towel, searching for slippers to hug her new clean feet. She forgot. She gritted her teeth at the imperfection, then clicked her tongue as if to say "tsk, tsk." You idiot, you forgot again. She spotted them nearby and tossed the towel on the floor, like a pathway to the soft slippers that awaited to hug her bare toes. She stepped onto the towel, reaching the slippers – and turned to toss the towel into the hamper.

Slam.

The house next door. Again.

She paused mid stride, dropped the towel. The dog yelped.

"Hector!" the woman yelled.

She clicked her tongue, but now her face became a solid mass of steel. Her jaw worked, and rage fluttered in her eyes as she parted the frilly curtains by her bed.

The heavyset polyester "maiden" was back again.

This time, she kicked the dog with a sneakered foot.

The dog cowered by the back fence as the woman took the dog's bowl and re-entered unseen.

Chevalie's eyes moistened with pity, but her rage worked her jaws tight. Two emotions in one face.

Quickly she dressed in a tee shirt with hearts and a pink hoodie and sweatpants printed with the Nike logo – and then sat at her desk, tying her sneakers.

Silence.

Chevalie pushed the textbooks aside, revealing the black hardbound book.

On the cover, a pentagram with a snake was embossed. The book appeared old and frayed, but sturdy like a brick.

"You bitch," she hissed.

Distracted by her own internal turmoil, she absently leafed quickly through the book, then slammed it shut. She darted to the clothes hamper, retrieved the wet towel she had just discarded, and turned it, inspecting it. Laying it flat on the wooden floor, she lay faceup on the towel, shimmying close to the bed. She reached under and grabbed a board. A game board of sorts, but it was not.

The board was homemade from a carton box, unfolded and cut. It was designed to be covered in felt, which Chevalie purchased at the fabric store downtown. She studied the home-sewn felt pockets, touching each one almost in a caress, all seven of them. There was a bulge in each pocket. What was inside each one was what was precious. And powerful.

She dipped her finger in one of the seven pockets of felt.

This particular one was labeled in some foreign symbol that was indecipherable. Her fingers revealed a ring with a blue gem. Sapphire. She examined it and placed it back into the felt pocket.

She reached for the notebook on her dresser and furiously wrote until she heard a car motor stop and a car door open.

She peered through her bedroom window at the driveway. A woman with strawberry-blonde hair in her forties exited a late-model Audi. The woman looked up and furrowed her brow and slammed the door shut. Chevalie ducked, hoping her mother had not seen her.

Quickly, Chevalie folded the felt-covered board and slid it under the bed, crumpling the wet towel. A draft announced the front door below opening.

"Chevy Lynn!"

Chevalie dashed to the hamper, tossed the towel and shut the closet door. She opened her bedroom door and dashed down the steps two at a time.

"Wassup, Mom?"

CHAPTER 3

Lynn Thayer stood in the foyer, clad in a navy blue tailored pants suit. She appeared irritated and pursed her lips as Chevalie descended.

"I told you to take the trash out this morning. Did you?"

"Good afternoon, Mom."

Lynn replied by straightening Chevalie's hoodie, though it appeared straight enough.

"How was school?"

"It's Memorial Day, remember?"

"Uh. Okay. Did you do chores or..."

"I studied for exams."

"I see. When are they?"

"Wednesday."

"Good. I'm tired. Closed two houses today."

Chevalie nodded, patiently waiting for a reprimand.

Lynn dug into her handbag. "I need you to run an errand for me at the local cleaners and then stop by the supermarket."

"Can I drive?"

"Of course not. You're not even fifteen yet. Here..."

Chevalie eyed the fifty-dollar bill and became pensive.

"Here's the list."

"I can't carry..."

"All that? Your bike's got a basket front and back like an old lady. Go. I have to cook."

Chevalie stuffed the money into her sweatshirt and looked down. "I need new jeans for summer. Everybody..."

"We'll shop when your brother gets home."

Chevalie's brother was already in college. She frowned, and anger swept her features again. Favored as the older brother, the goodnik, the poster-boy son, the entire summer would be spent again, she thought, currying to his needs.

"What are you waiting for?"

Chevalie dashed out the front door and walked to the side of the house where her old bicycle leaned against the fence. Anger bloomed in her heart, like a flock of crows taking flight. She spotted the large black Hefty bag – the trash – and realized she forgot to take it to the curb. Her anger dropped, replaced by anxiety. Her stomach fluttered. She grabbed the large Hefty bag, and visions of the dead cat hours earlier in a white bag and tie next door flashed before her.

She turned, looked back at the house and saw her mother through the kitchen window, filling a teapot with water, her back to Chevalie.

Quickly now, Chevalie grabbed the trash bag with one hand and the bicycle bars in the other. She darted towards the curb, straining with her load, and spotted the white tied bag on the curb outside the Scott's house, waiting for the next morning's pickup. The dead cat. She approached with both hands grasping the large black Hefty and plopped it right next to the bag where the dead cat lay inside.

She grabbed the bag with the dead cat, watching the front windows of the widow, Edith. No one. She dashed to the front door and untied the bag, wrinkling her nose as she peered inside.

She poured the dead cat, now stiff, on Edith's front doormat.

She heard Hector whine inside the house, looked at the nearby window and saw him looking out, watching her.

She put one finger up as if to signal to wait. The dog panted, tongue out, tail wagging. Chevalie turned away, ran down the steps and grabbed her bicycle, pedaling furiously down the street. As she pedaled, she surveyed the neighborhood, a grin on her face.

CHAPTER 4

Mrs. Scott walked out the back door, carrying freshly cooked ground turkey still steaming in the dog's bowl. She exuded a look of guilt mixed with pity for nudging Hector perhaps too hard: the only remaining memory of her deceased husband. Two years had gone by, and the last present from him was the brown lab, a puppy at the time. Now Hector was two, whining, it appeared, for having lost his friend Chia, the sixteen-year-old orange cat.

The screen door screeched as she opened it with her elbow. It needed oiling, like the rest of the old house; the gutter and the garden needed mending. She knew she was getting old, and her son wanted her to move closer to him, but she loved Connecticut. Unlike Fort Lauderdale with its eternal summers and humidity, crocodiles and mosquitos, not to mention the change of supermarkets and shopping places, she wanted to remain where she was most comfortable. It was home where she was. She held the screen door, called out to Hector, and he emerged from the living room, where he was looking out the window, watching and whining intently. Why, she had no idea, but would have to investigate if the mailman, Ralph, was out there. She looked forward to his visits, as he was a former high school chum of her husband. He didn't look that bad, she thought. She knew Ralph was a widower.

The dog lapped at the boiled turkey, wagging his tail, and Edith Scott was happy. In her mind, it made up for nudging him with her foot and blaming him for not watching Chia more closely. How could he? He was only a dog, and dogs do what dogs do. Play. When the cat began to slow down, she dreaded the day Chia would need to be put down, and coming home to tell Hector Chia wasn't coming back.

However, the grace of God provided, and she, actually Hector, had found Chia dead. He'd whined and howled like a wolf in mourning, and she'd looked out the window to see what was up. Shocked but relieved she didn't have to bring her end, she couldn't bring herself to bury the cat, let alone take her to the vet for a cremation. How much would it cost? She dialed the phone, hoping she could afford it; then the sweet voice of the new veterinary assistant came on to tell her they had a discount on cremations. When she queried about the fee, she almost had a stroke. *Well*, Edith thought, *what can I do...* so she emerged with a kitchen bag, which she had put catnip in for Chia to enjoy in the nether life, and placed her in the bag before Hector had a chance to do what dogs usually do... play with dead things. Thank goodness Chia wasn't a squirrel. He would have torn her apart, as he was an intelligent and curious dog.

As she watched him finish his food with gusto, she walked to the side of the house that separated her from the Conners next door, who had a wrought-iron fence. Very pretty and upscale, matching their Georgian house with the black gables and six-bedroom red-brick home. She gave the house a cursory glance, already knowing it was perfect, unlike her home, which she felt appeared shabby and small in comparison, even though it was a vintage Victorian.

Edith sauntered up front, surveyed the street in her customary way to take in who was already out. She paused on the sidewalk, not meaning to stare as the mailman walked towards her house. She smiled inwardly, appearing coy and not too anxious. She noted the Thayer girl with the first name of a car was already on her bike, pedaling furiously away, undoubtedly off from school or playing hooky. She recalled the mother was a Realtor, which would come in handy if she chose to move.

Trying to find an excuse to linger outside, she looked at her bushes, as if to inspect the hydrangeas she'd forgotten to prune last winter, as Ralph approached, mailbag filled with the trappings of his trade. Then, as he got closer, he pulled out her mail, junk and all. He was in the act of handing it to her instead of placing it in her mailbox – when his smile turned down at the corners.

He froze as his glance gave way to a stare past Edith. "Hey, Edith. Don't mean to pry."

Edith chuckled uncomfortably, her hand straying to her spring coat, which was partially open to reveal her housedress. "Shoot, Ralph."

"What's that on your doorstep?"

∼

Coming from Beyond The Fray Publishing: More true horror from the author of THE WAY THROUGH THE WOODS and HAUNTED HEIRLOOMS.

On Amazon where books are sold.

ABOUT THE AUTHOR

Therapist, award-winning screenwriter and travel photographer, Anna Maria Manalo is a creative nonfiction author of supernatural suspense novels and anthologies. All her books are rated at 4.3 to 4.8 on Amazon, all based on first-person accounts.

Anna has amassed paranormal encounters from all over the globe as an artist and traveller. Her cinematic storytelling style and characters based on real individuals brings books that fully immerse the reader in the experience of the phenomena as she takes them into terrifying landscapes.

Her writing has been likened to Isabelle Allende and Elie Wiesel.

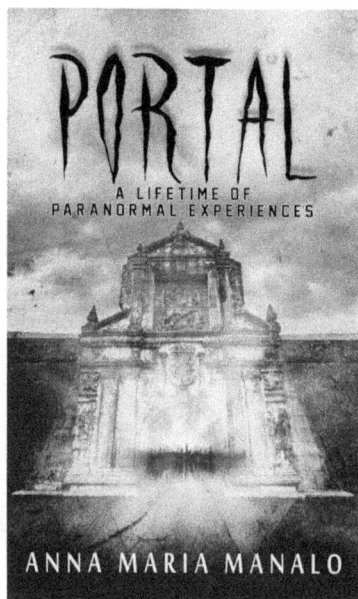

Portal: A Lifetime of Paranormal Experiences

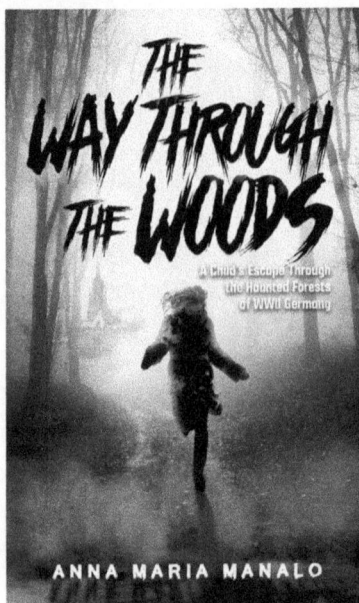

The Way Through the Woods: A Child's Escape Through the Haunted Forests of WWII Germany